GCSE
French
GRAMMAR GUIDE

Elaine Harnick
Terry Murray

EDUCATIONAL

Every effort has been made to trace copyright holders and to obtain their permission for the use of copyright material. The authors and publishers will gladly receive information enabling them to rectify any error or omission in subsequent editions.

First published 1998

Letts Educational,
Schools and Colleges Division,
9–15 Aldine Street,
London W12 8AW
Tel   0181 740 2270
Fax   0181 740 2280

Text © Elaine Harnick & Terry Murray 1998

Editorial, design and production by Moondisks Ltd, Cambridge

All our rights reserved. No part of this publication may be reproduced, stored in a retrieval system, or transmitted, in any form or by any means, electronic, mechanical, photocopying, recording or otherwise, without prior permission of Letts Educational.

British Library Cataloguing-in-Publication Data
A CIP record for this book is available from the British Library

ISBN 1 84085 082 5

Printed and bound in Great Britain

Letts Educational is the trading name of BPP (Letts Educational) Ltd

For Stella

Contents

Contents

Introduction

This book is a systematic guide to all the grammar required for the GCSE examinations of all the UK examination boards. The authors have aimed to provide a simple, guided approach to grammar points, alerting users to particular 'problem areas'. The straightforward exercises contained in each section give the opportunity for practice, and independent users can check their answers with those provided at the end of the book.

Essential words

Les jours de la semaine	The days of the week
lundi	Monday
mardi	Tuesday
mercredi	Wednesday
jeudi	Thursday
vendredi	Friday
samedi	Saturday
dimanche	Sunday

Les mois de l'année	The months of the year
janvier	January
février	February
mars	March
avril	April
mai	May
juin	June
juillet	July
août	August
septembre	September
octobre	October
novembre	November
décembre	December

Les nombres cardinaux   Cardinal numbers

0	*zéro*	20	*vingt*
1	*un/une*	21	*vingt et un*
2	*deux*	22	*vingt-deux*
3	*trois*	30	*trente*
4	*quatre*	40	*quarante*
5	*cinq*	50	*cinquante*
6	*six*	60	*soixante*
7	*sept*	70	*soixante-dix*
8	*huit*	71	*soixante et onze*
9	*neuf*	80	*quatre-vingts*
10	*dix*	90	*quatre-vingt-dix*
11	*onze*	100	*cent*
12	*douze*	101	*cent un*
13	*treize*	190	*cent quatre-vingt-dix*
14	*quatorze*	200	*deux cents*
15	*quinze*	211	*deux cent onze*
16	*seize*	1000	*mille*
17	*dix-sept*	2000	*deux mille*
18	*dix-huit*	1000 000	*un million*
19	*dix-neuf*		

Les nombres ordinaux — Ordinal numbers

premier (masc.) *première* (fem.)	first
deuxième	second
troisième	third
quatrième	fourth
cinquième	fifth
sixième	sixth
septième	seventh
huitième	eighth
neuvième	ninth
dixième	tenth
onzième	eleventh

L'heure (fem.) — The time

Quelle heure est-il?	What's the time?
Il est sept heures.	It's seven o'clock.
Il est deux heures cinq.	It's five past two.
Il est neuf heures et quart.	It's a quarter past nine.
Il est quatre heures et demie.	It's half past four.
Il est six heures moins vingt.	It's twenty to six.
Il est une heure moins le quart.	It's a quarter to one.
Il est midi/minuit.	It's twelve o'clock noon/midnight.
Il est midi et demi.	It's half past twelve (noon).
Il est minuit et demie.	It's half past twelve (midnight)
A seize heures vingt-cinq	At 16.25
A quatorze heures quarante-cinq	At 14.45

2

A dix-huit heures	At 18.00
du matin	a.m.
de l'après-midi	p.m. until 5p.m.
du soir	p.m. after 5p.m.
à cinq heures du matin	at five o'clock in the morning

Quelle est la date d'aujourd'hui?	What's the date today?
C'est lundi treize janvier mille neuf cent quatre-vingt-seize OR *dix-neuf cent quatre-vingt-seize*	It's Monday the thirteenth of January 1996.
Le dimanche premier mai	Sunday, the first of May

Les saisons (fem.)	The seasons
le printemps	spring
l'été (masc.)	summer
l'automne (masc.)	autumn
l'hiver (masc.)	winter
au printemps	in spring
en été/automne/hiver	in summer/autumn/winter
pendant l'été	during the summer

Les interrogatifs (masc.)	Question Words
à quelle heure?	at what time?
à qui?	whose?
avec qui?	with whom?
combien de fois?	how many times? = how often?
combien de temps?	how long?
combien?	how much, how many?
comment ... ?	how?
où?	where?
pourquoi?	why?
qu'est-ce que?	what?
qu'est-ce qui?	what?
quand?	when?
qui est-ce qui?	who?
qui?	who?
quoi?	what?

1 Grammatical terms

Before you start your grammar revision, you need to familiarise yourself with some grammatical terms. Look at this sentence:

The boy eats a delicious dinner slowly in the kitchen.

The	definite article
boy	noun (subject)
eats	verb
a	indefinite article
delicious	adjective
dinner	noun (direct object)
slowly	adverb
in	preposition
the	definite article
kitchen.	noun

▨ The **definite article** is the grammatical name given to the word **the**.

▨ The **indefinite article** is the name given to the word **a** or **an**.

▨ A **noun** is a person, place, thing or animal, e.g. **Tom, London, chair, cat.**

▨ A **verb** is a word that describes an action, e.g. **eats**.

▨ An **adjective** is a word that describes a noun, e.g **delicious**.

▨ An **adverb** is a word that describes a verb. It tells you how an action is done, e.g. **slowly**. Many adverbs in English end in **-ly**.

▨ A **preposition** is a word placed before a noun or a pronoun to indicate time, place or condition, e.g. **in** the kitchen.

▨ A **conjunction** is a word that links two parts of a sentence, e.g. he was eating **and** drinking. The most common conjunctions in English are **and** and **but**.

▨ A **pronoun** is a word that stands in place of a noun. In the sentence above, we could replace the noun **the boy** by the pronoun **he**. Similarly, **a dinner** could be replaced by **it**.

▨ A **relative pronoun** is a word that links one part of a sentence to another. In English the relative pronouns are **who, whom, which, that**, e.g. I gave him all the money **that** I earned. The two parts of the sentence, **I gave him all the money** and **I earned**, are linked together by the relative pronoun **that**.

▓ A **negative** is a word like **not** or **never** that indicates an action is not being done.

▓ **Gender** refers to whether a word is masculine or feminine.

▓ The **subject** is the name given to the person or thing doing the action. In the sentence above, the subject is **the boy**.

▓ The **direct object** is the name given to the person or thing that has the action done directly to it. In the sentence above, **a dinner** is the object because it is eaten by the boy.

Q 1 **The French Minister unexpectedly came to Britain.**

a What is the subject?

_____

b Find the verb.

_____

c Find an adjective.

_____

d Find an adverb.

_____

He took a flight yesterday and the Prime Minister met him in London.

e Find a pronoun.

_____

f Find a preposition.

_____

g Find three nouns.

_____

_____

_____

h Find a conjunction

_____

2 The indefinite article

This is the grammatical way of referring to **a** or **an**.

In English we use **a** before a consonant and **an** before a vowel,

e.g.   **a** boy   **an** elephant

In French we use **un** before a masculine noun, we use **une** before a feminine noun,

e.g.   **un** *homme*   **a** man
       un *chat*   **a** cat
       une *femme*   **a** woman
       une *chatte*   **a** female cat

To a is *à un* … or *à une* …

e.g.   *Je suis allé à un concert et à une boum.*
       I went **to a** concert and **to a** party.

Of a is *d'un* … or *d'une* …

e.g.   *a page d'un livre*   the page **of a** book
       la page d'une revue   the page **of a** magazine

Points to watch

Leave out **un** and **une** when stating a person's job,

e.g.   *Il est facteur.*   He is **a** postman.

Leave out **un** and **une** before *cent* and *mille*,

e.g.   *cent livres*   **a** hundred books
       mille livres   **a** thousand books

Q 2   **Write in French.**

a   a cat, a house, a field, a boy, a girl, an apple, an egg

_____

_____

b   He sells to a supermarket and to a bakery.

_____

_____

c   the garden of a house, the garden of a castle

_____

_____

d I am a teacher.

_____

e a hundred pens and a thousand pencils.

_____

_____

3 The definite article

This is the grammatical way of referring to **the**.

There are **four** ways of saying **the** in French:

a *le* in front of a masculine singular noun,

e.g.	*le garçon*	**the** boy
	le champ	**the** field
	le livre	**the** book

b *la* in front of a feminine singular noun,

e.g.	*la fille*	**the** girl
	la chaise	**the** chair
	la mère	**the** mother

c *l'* in front of a singular noun that begins with a vowel or a silent *h*,

e.g.	*l'enfant*	**the** child
	l'eau	**the** water
	l'animal	**the** animal

d *les* in front of any plural noun,

e.g.	*les garçons*	**the** boys
	les animaux	**the** animals
	les eaux	**the** waters

To say **to the** in French you can say *à la , à l'*.

You <u>**cannot**</u> say *à + le*, you must say *au*.

You <u>**cannot**</u> say *à + les*, you must say *aux*.

e.g.	*Je vais au marché.*	I am going **to the** market.
	Je vais à la boulangerie.	I am going **to the** bakery.
	Je vais à l'aéroport.	I am going **to the** airport.
	Je vais aux magasins.	I am going **to the** shops.

To say **of the** you can say *de la* and *de l'*.

You <u>**cannot**</u> say *de + le*, you must say *du*.

You <u>**cannot**</u> say *de + les*, you must say *des*.

e.g. *le fils du roi*   **the** king's son (the son **of the** king)
la fille de la reine   **the** queen's daughter
                      (the daughter **of the** queen)
la porte de l'église   ·the door **of the** church
les livres des enfants   **the** children's books

Points to watch

The is used in French when we leave it out in English:

a when you are talking about something in a general sense,

e.g. *J'aime le vin.*   I like wine.
Je déteste l'histoire.   I hate history.

b with countries and languages,

e.g. *La France est belle.*   France is beautiful.
L'anglais est plus difficile que le français.
English is more difficult than French.

c when speaking about the parts of the body,

e.g. *J'ai les yeux bleus.*   I have blue eyes.
Je me lave les mains.   I wash my hands.

d when using people's titles,

e.g. *Le rois Charles*   King Charles
Le général de Gaulle   General De Gaulle

Q 3   **Write in French.**

a the pen, the pencil, the sister, the daughter, the son, the window, the friend, the child, the hotel, the pens, the sisters, the friends, the hotels.

_____

_____

_____

b Cats are interesting, but dogs are more interesting.

_____

_____

c French is the language of Belgium.

_____

_____

d She has long hair.

_____

e Queen Elizabeth

_____

f I am going to the cinema; I am going to the hotel; I am going to the shops; I am going to the butcher's.

_____

_____

_____

_____

g the man's pen, the woman's pen, the boy's pen, the boys' pens

_____

_____

4 The partitive article

This is the grammatical way of referring to **some/any**.

a *Du* is used before masculine singular nouns,

    e.g. *Je voudrais du jambon.*   I would like **some** ham.

b *De la* is used before feminine singular nouns,

    e.g. *Je voudrais de la bière.*   I would like **some** beer.

c *De l'* is used before singular nouns beginning with a vowel,

    e.g. *Je voudrais de l' argent.*   I would like **some** money.

d *Des* is used before all plural nouns,

    e.g. *Je voudrais des oignons.*   I would like **some** onions.

Points to watch

There are three occasions when *du, de la, de l'* and *des* are not used. Instead you use *de* or *d'*.

a after an expression of quantity/measures,

e.g.
un litre de vin	a litre of wine
un kilo d'oranges	a kilo of oranges
un peu de beurre	a little butter
beaucoup d'argent	a lot of money
assez de problèmes	enough problems

b after a **negative,** i.e. after *ne...pas,*

e.g.
Je ne veux pas de pain.	I don't want any bread.
Je n'ai pas d'amis.	I have no friends.
Je ne vois pas d'arbres.	I don't see any trees.

c when you have an adjective that comes before a plural noun,

e.g.
de beaux garçons	handsome boys
de belles femmes	beautiful women
de grands magasins	big shops

Q 4 **Write in French.**

a I buy some bread, some wine, some meat, some jam, some water and some apples.

_____

_____

_____

b I eat a little meat and a lot of fruit.

_____

_____

c I bought a litre of oil and 500 grammes of cheese.

_____

_____

d I would like some coffee but I do not want any milk.

_____

_____

e I have some money but I haven't got a car.

_____

_____

f I can see some tourists but I do not see any students.

_____

_____

5 Gender of nouns

All nouns in French are either masculine or feminine. When you learn a noun you must learn its gender, i.e. whether it is masculine or feminine.

Here are some tips to help you learn the gender of nouns.

a Male people are usually masculine, female people are usually feminine,

e.g. *le frère* (brother) but *la sœur* (sister), *le père* (father) but *la mère* (mother), *le grand-père* (grandfather) but *la grand-mère* (grandmother).

b When the noun is a thing or an idea there is no obvious pattern to help you. You must learn each word individually,

e.g. *le chapeau*   hat
      la cravate   tie
      le livre   book
      la voiture   car

c Some words are either masculine or feminine depending on whether you are talking about a male or a female,

e.g. *un artiste* or *une artiste*   artist
      un élève or *une élève*   pupil
      un touriste or *une touriste*   tourist

d Some words do not change their gender. They are always either masculine or feminine no matter whether they refer to a man or a woman,

e.g. *une victime*   victim (man or woman)
      un professeur teacher (man or woman)
      un médecin   doctor (man or woman)

e The following are masculine:

▦ the days, the months, the seasons,

  e.g.   *le mardi*   on Tuesdays
      le printemps   spring

▦ languages,

  e.g.   *le français*   French
      le chinois   Chinese

▦ countries not ending in *-e*

  e.g.   *le Canada, le Portugal* (but most countries end in *-e* and are feminine [one exception is *le Mexique*, Mexico])

▦ points of the compass,

  e.g.   *le nord*   north

f If you see a noun with one of the following endings, it is usually masculine:

-age	e.g.	*le village*	village
		le fromage	cheese
-ain	e.g.	*le terrain*	ground
		le copain	friend
-eau	e.g.	*le tableau*	picture
		le château	castle
-eur	e.g.	*l'agriculteur*	farmer
		l'instituteur	primary school teacher
-ien	e.g.	*le chien*	dog
		le pharmacien	chemist
- ier	e.g.	*le fermier*	farmer
		le métier	job
-ment	e.g.	*le mouvement*	movement
		le gouvernement	government
-oir	e.g.	*le trottoir*	pavement
		le couloir	corridor

g If you see a noun with the following endings it is usually feminine:

- ance	e.g.	***La*** France	France
		la chance	luck
- ée	e.g.	*la matinée*	morning
		l'entrée	entrance

- ence e.g.	*l'agence*	agency
	la résidence	residence
- ette e.g.	*la cigarette*	cigarette
	l'allumette	match
- ie e.g.	*la mairie*	town hall
	la sortie	exit
- ion e.g.	*l'instruction*	instruction
	l'équitation	horse-riding

h Some nouns change their meanings when they change gender,

e.g.	*le livre*	book	*la livre*	a pound
	le poste	job	*la poste*	post office
	le tour	tour	*la tour*	tower

Q 5 Are the following nouns masculine or feminine? Learn the rules in Section 5 and apply them to these words.

a *cousin* _____

b *cousine* _____

c *propiétaire* (man) _____

d *propiétaire* (woman) _____

e *chef* _____

f *lundi* _____

g *été* _____

h *l'espagnol* _____

i *sud* _____

j *canotage* _____

k *bain* _____

l *rideau* _____

m *conducteur* _____

n *mécanicien* _____

o *sanglier* _____

p *changement* _____

q *pouvoir* _____

r *distance* _____

s *journée* _____

t *négligence* _____

u *chaussette* _____

v *maladie* _____

w *distraction* _____

Write in French.

x a book and a pound

_____

_____

y a job at the post-office

_____

_____

z a tour of the tower

_____

_____

6 Plural of nouns

In English to make a noun plural you add -s. In French you do the same. However:

a Words that end in *-s*, *-x*, or *-z* do not change in the plural,

    e.g. **le** *temps*   the time   **les** *temps*   the times
         la *voix*   the voice   **les** *voix*   the voices
         le *nez*   the nose   **les** *nez*   the noses

b Words that end in *-al* change to *-aux* in the plural.
   Words that end in *-ou* sometimes just add *-s*,

    e.g. **le** *trou*   the hole   **les** *trous*   the holes

   but sometimes add *-x*. See the examples overleaf.

c Words that end in *-eau* or *-eu* add *-x* to make the plural. See the examples overleaf. An exception is *le pneu* the tyre, **les** *pneus* the tyres.

Here is a list of plurals that you need to know.

singular	plural	
l'animal (m)	**les** animau**x**	animal(**s**)
le bijou	**les** bijou**x**	jewel(**s**)
le bois	**les** bois	wood(**s**)
le cadeau	**les** cadeau**x**	present(**s**)
le caillou	**les** caillou**x**	pebble(**s**)
le chapeau	**les** chapeau**x**	hat(**s**)
le château	**les** château**x**	castle(**s**)
le cheval	**les** chevau**x**	horse(**s**)
le chou	**les** chou**x**	cabbage(**s**)
le ciel	**les** cieu**x**	sky/heaven, skies/heavens
l'eau (f)	**les** eau**x**	water(**s**)
le feu	**les** feu**x**	fire(**s**) (pl. also = traffic-lights)
le fils	**les** fils	son(**s**)
le gâteau	**les** gâteau**x**	cake(**s**)
le genou	**les** genou**x**	knee(**s**)
le hibou	**les** hibou**x**	owl(**s**)
le jeu	**les** jeu**x**	game(**s**)
le journal	**les** journau**x**	newspaper(**s**)
le mal	**les** mau**x**	evil(**s**)/harm(**s**)/hurt(**s**)
le nez	**les** nez	nose(**s**)
l'œil (m)	**les** yeu**x**	eye(**s**)
l'oiseau	**les** oiseau**x**	bird(**s**)
l'os (m)	**les** os	bone(**s**)
le prix	**les** pri**x**	price(**s**)/prize(**s**)
le tableau	**les** tableau**x**	picture(**s**)
le temps	**les** temps	time(**s**)/weather(**s**)
le travail	**les** travau**x**	works

Note also:

madame	**mes**dames	
madememoiselle	**mes**demoiselles	
monsieur	**mes**sieurs	

Point to watch

Family names do not change in French when they are used in the plural,

e.g. *Nous allons chez **les Torcq**.* We are going to **the Torcqs.**

Q 6   **Write in French.**

1   the time, the times

_____

2   the voice, the voices

_____

3   the nose, the noses

_____

4   the hole, the holes

_____

5   the tyre, the tyres

_____

6   the animal, the animals

_____

7   the jewel, the jewels

_____

8   the wood, the woods

_____

9   the pebble, the pebbles

_____

10   the hat, the hats

_____

11   the castle, the castles

_____

12   the horse, the horses

_____

13   the cabbage, the cabbages

_____

14   the heaven, the heavens

_____

15   the water, the waters

_____

16 the fire, the fires

_____

17 the cake, the cakes

_____

18 the knee, the knees

_____

19 the owl, the owls

_____

20 the game, the games

_____

21 the newspaper, the newspapers

_____

22 the evil, the evils

_____

23 the eye, the eyes

_____

24 the bird, the birds

_____

25 the bone, the bones

_____

26 the price, the prices

_____

27 the picture, the pictures

_____

28 the stamp, the stamps

_____

29 the work, the works

_____

30 young ladies! Ladies! Gentlemen

_____

_____

> 31 We are going to eat at the Smiths.
>
> _____

7 Agreement of adjectives

An **adjective** is a word that describes a noun or a pronoun,

    e.g. a **blue** car.

Blue describes the car so blue is an **adjective**.

Agreement means that with French adjectives sometimes you have to add *-e* or *-s* or *-es* to the end of the adjective. (See below.)

a If an adjective describes a feminine singular noun, add *-e*.
    If an adjective describes a masculine plural noun, add *-s*.
    If an adjective describes a feminine plural noun, add *-es*.

      e.g.   *un livre **bleu*****   a **blue** book
               *une chaise **bleue***   a **blue** chair
               *deux livres **bleus***   two **blue** books
               *deux chaises **bleues*** two **blue** chairs

b If the adjective ends in *-e* already (e.g. ***rouge***), do not add another *-e*,

      e.g.   *un livre **rouge***   a **red** chair
               *une chaise **rouge***   a **red** chair
               *deux livres **rouges*** two **red** books
               *deux chaises **rouges*** two **red** chairs

c If an adjective ends in *-s* already (e.g. ***gris***), do not add another *-s*,

      e.g.   *un livre **gris***   a **grey** book
               *deux livres **gris*** two **grey** books

d Adjectives that end in *-eux* change to *-euse* in the feminine,

      e.g.   *un garçon **heureux***   a **happy** boy
               *une fille **heureuse***   a **happy** girl
               *deux garçons **heureux*** two **happy** boys
               *deux filles **heureuses*** two **happy** girls

e Look how adjectives that end in *-if, -oux, -ien, -er, -il* change in the feminine,

      e.g.   *un garçon **sportif***   an **athletic** boy
               *une fille **sportive***   an **athletic** girl
               *un garçon **jaloux***   a **jealous** boy
               *une fille **jalouse***   a **jealous** girl
               *un garçon **italien***   an **Italian** boy
               *une fille **italienne*** an **Italian** girl

*le **premier** garçon*	the **first** boy
*la **première** fille*	the **first** girl
*un **gentil** garçon*	a **nice** boy
*une **gentille** fille*	a **nice** girl

Q 7 **Write in French.**

a a brown book

_____

b a brown chair

_____

c two brown books

_____

d two brown chairs

_____

e two enormous chairs

_____

f two English boys

_____

g a lazy girl

_____

h two lazy boys

_____

i an active boy

_____

j an active girl

_____

k an ancient house

_____

l an expensive shirt

_____

m a similar situation

_____

8 Irregular adjectives

Here is a list of adjectives with difficult feminine forms.

masculine singular	feminine singular		masculine singular	feminine singular	
ancien	**ancienne**	old	gentil	**gentille**	nice
bas	**basse**	low	gras	**grasse**	fat
beau	**belle**	beautiful	gros	**grosse**	big
blanc	**blanche**	white	jaloux	**jalouse**	jealous
bon	**bonne**	good	long	**longue**	long
bref	**brève**	brief	neuf	**neuve**	brand new
cher	**chère**	dear	nouveau	**nouvelle**	new
doux	**douce**	sweet	premier	**première**	first
épais	**épaisse**	thick	public	**publique**	public
entier	**entière**	entire/whole	roux	**rousse**	auburn, russet
faux	**fausse**	false	sec	**sèche**	dry
favori	**favorite**	favourite	secret	**secrète**	secret
fou	**folle**	mad	vieux	**vieille**	old
frais	**fraîche**	fresh	vif	**vive**	lively

Note also the forms **bel, nouvel, vieil**. These are used before masculine singular words beginning with a vowel or **h**,

e.g.   *un **bel** homme, un **nouvel** élève, un **vieil** autobus*
a **handsome** man, a **new** pupil, an **old** bus

Q 8   **Write in French.**

a   a low ceiling

_____

b   a beautiful woman

_____

c   two white houses

_____

d   a thick slice

_____

e   the whole family

_____

f   a favourite subject

_____

g two fresh strawberiries

_____

h a fat cat (female)

_____

i two large boxes

_____

j a long walk

_____

k a brand new car

_____

l a dry towel

_____

m an old story

_____

n a lively girl

_____

o a new friend

_____

9 Position of adjectives

In French the adjective usually comes after the noun. The French name the item and then describe it. These common adjectives however come **before** the noun.

beau (beautiful)	*bon* (good)	*excellent* (excellent)
gentil (nice)	*grand* (big)	*gros* (big/fat)
jeune (young)	*joli* (pretty)	*long* (long)
mauvais (bad)	*même* (same)	*meilleur* (better/best)
nouveau (new)	*petit* (small)	*vieux* (old)
vilain (nasty)		

Point to watch

Some adjectives change their meaning according to their position:

un *cher* ami	a **dear** friend
un vin *cher*	an **expensive** wine
un *ancien* élève	a **former** pupil
un bâtiment *ancien*	an **old** building
mes *propres* mains	my **own** hands
mes mains *propres*	my **clean** hands

Q 9 **Write in French.**

a an excellent match

_____

b a young man

_____

c a bad boy

_____

d the same thing

_____

e his best friend

_____

f a small glass

_____

g the old bridge

_____

h my dear nephew

_____

i my expensive car

_____

j my own house

_____

k my clean house

_____

10 Six useful adjectives

a *Autre(s)*   other

Les *autres* élèves sont sages.	The **other** pupils are good.
J'ai une *autre* robe rouge.	I have **another** red dress.

b *Chaque*   each

chaque élève	**each** pupil
chaque maison	**each** house

c *Même(s)*   same

Nous avons vu le *même* film.	We saw the **same** film.
Ils ont les *mêmes* CDs.	They have the **same** CDs.

d *Plusieurs*   several

J'ai acheté *plusieurs* livres.	I have bought **several** books.

e *Quelque(s)*   some

pendant *quelque* temps	for **some** time
Quelques élèves sont arrivés.	**Some** pupils have arrived.

f **Tel, telle, tels, telles   such**

Pay special attention to the position of this word.

Un *tel* homme ne le ferait.	**Such** a man (a man like that) would not do it.
Une *telle* femme ne le ferait.	**Such** a woman (a woman like that) would not do it.
De *tels* hommes ne le feraient.	**Such** men (men like that) would not do it.
De *telles* femmes ne le feraient.	**Such** women (women like that) would not do it.

g *Tout, toute, tous, toutes*   all (+ article)

tout le fromage	**all** the cheese
toute la famille	**all** the family
tous les garçons	**all** the boys
toutes les jeunes filles	**all** the girls

Q 10   Write in French.

a another friend

_____

b Each child has the same book.

_____

_____

c several times

_____

d some books

_____

e Such children (children like that) are rare.

_____

_____

f all the nieces and all the nephews

_____

_____

11 Comparative and superlative of adjectives

We use the comparative to compare two people or things, e.g. John's car is **bigger** than mine. We use the superlative for three or more people or things, e.g. Mary is the **tallest** girl in the class.

a The comparative and superlative forms of adjectives are quite simple when the adjective precedes the noun:

Comparative:
plus   **more,**

   e.g. *plus jeune*   **young**er

moins **less,**

   e.g. *moins jeune*   **less** young/**not as** young

aussi **as,**

   e.g. *aussi jeune*   **as** young

Superlative:
le (la, les) plus   **the most,**

   e.g. *le plus jeune*   **the** young**est**

le (la, les) moins the least,

   e.g. *le moins jeune*   **the least** young

In the comparative, *que* is used to complete the comparison. It can mean **as** or **than**:

> e.g. *Pierre est **plus jeune que** Jean.*
> Peter is **younger than** John.
> *Les lions sont **aussi beaux que** les tigres.*
> Lions are **as beautiful as** tigers.

Be careful with:
meilleur   **better,**

> e.g. *un **meilleur** élève*   a **better** pupil

le meilleur   **the best,**

> e.g. *le **meilleur** élève*   the **best** pupil

b When an adjective follows the noun, it keeps the same position when it is made comparative or superlative,

> e.g. *une histoire **plus** amusante*   a more interesting story

In the superlative, the definite article must be repeated after the noun,

> e.g. *l'histoire **la plus** amusante*   the most interesting story

c **In** with a superlative is translated by *de*,

> e.g. *L'élève le plus intelligent **de** la classe.*
> The most intelligent pupil **in** the class.

Q 11   Write in French.

a The green car is bigger than the blue car.

_____

_____

b The blue car is less expensive.

_____

_____

c The red car is the biggest.

_____

_____

d The white car is as expensive as the green car.

_____

_____

e The grey car is the least expensive.

_____

_____

f The red car is the most expensive.

_____

_____

g The best car is a French car.

_____

_____

h French cars are better than English cars.

_____

_____

i The most important thing is the price.

_____

_____

j French cars are the best in the world.

_____

_____

12 Demonstrative adjectives

Demonstrative adjectives mean **this** or **these**, **that** or **those**.

masculine	feminine	plural
ce	*cette*	*ces*

Point to watch

There is a special masculine singular form which is used before a vowel or *h*: *cet,*

e.g. *cet homme*

These adjectives correspond to the English **this, that/these, those,**

e.g. *ce livre*   **this** book, **that** book
      cet homme   **this** man, **that** man
      cette maison **this** house, **that** house
      ces élèves   **these** pupils, **those** pupils

-ci and *-là* may be added for extra emphasis,

e.g. *ce livre-ci*   **this** book (here)
      ce livre-là   **that** book (there), etc.

Q 12 Write in French.

a this chair

_____

b this dog

_____

c this friend (boy)

_____

d this friend (girl)

_____

e these chairs

_____

f this chair (here)

_____

g that chair (there)

_____

h these chairs (here)

_____

i those chairs (there)

_____

13 Possessive adjectives

Possessive adjectives show who something belongs to, e.g. **my** coat, **his** hair, **their** holidays.

	masculine	feminine	plural
my	*mon*	*ma*	*mes*
your	*ton*	*ta*	*tes*
his/her/its	*son*	*sa*	*ses*
our	*notre*	*notre*	*nos*
your	*votre*	*votre*	*vos*
their	*leur*	*leur*	*leurs*

a Use *mon*, *ton* or *son* etc if the word following it is masculine singular,

   e.g. *mon chien*   **my** dog

Use **ma, ta, sa**, etc if the word following it is feminine singular,

   e.g. *ma maison*   **my** house

Use **mes, tes, ses**, etc if the word following it is plural,

   e.g. *mes livres*   **my** books

b The difference in usage depends on the gender of the person or thing owned and not on the gender of the owner,

   e.g. *sa maman*   **his** mother or **her** mother
        son stylo   **his** pen or **her** pen.

Points to watch

a Before a singular feminine noun beginning with a vowel or *h*, use **mon, ton, son**,

   e.g. *son amie*   **his (her)** girlfriend
        ton histoire   **your** story
        mon auto   **my** car

Q 13   Write in French.

a my dog

_____

b my dogs

_____

c my chair

_____

d my idea

_____

e your dog

_____

f your dogs

_____

g your chair

_____

h your intention

_____

i his dog

_____

j her dog

_____

k his dogs

_____

l her dogs

_____

m our car

_____

n our cars

_____

o your car

_____

p your cars

_____

q their house

_____

r their houses

_____

14 Interrogative adjectives

Interrogative adjectives are the question words we use to ask **which?** or **what?**

Look at these examples.

Quel livre? (masc. sing.)	**Which** book?
Quelle chaise? (fem. sing.)	**Which** chair?
Quels livres? (masc. pl.)	**Which** books?
Quelles chaises? (fem. pl.)	**Which** chairs?

These adjectives can also be used in exclamations such as:

Quelle journée!	**What** a day!
Quel temps!	**What** weather!

Q 14 Write in French.

a Which dog?

_____

b Which dogs?

_____

c Which page?

_____

d Which pages?

_____

e What's your name?

_____

f What is your phone number?

_____

g What a pity!

_____

15 Adverbs

Adverbs are words that give more information about a verb, an adjective or another adverb,

> e.g.   He walks **quickly**.   The scarves are **brightly** coloured.

a A lot of adverbs end in **-ly** in English. **-ly** in English is usually *-ment* in French,

> e.g.   *rapide*   quick
> *rapide**ment***   quick**ly**
> *général*   general
> *générale**ment*** general**ly**

b To form an adverb, add *-ment* to the **feminine** form of the adjective,

> e.g.   sweet is *doux* (masc.), *douce* (fem.), so
> sweet**ly** is douce*ment*.

c If the adjective ends in a vowel, add *-ment* to the masculine form of the adjective,

> e.g.   *vrai*   **true**
> *vrai**ment***   tru**ly**

d Never add *-ment* to *vite*,

> e.g.   *vite*   quickly

e Not all adverbs end in *-ment*,

> e.g.   *souvent*   often
> *beaucoup*   a lot
> *trop*   too much
> *vite*   quickly
> *tout à fait* completely

f Watch out when using these five adverbs with a perfect tense: the adverb comes before the past participle.

> *Je suis **souvent** allé en France.*   I **often** went to France.
> *J'ai **beaucoup** mangé.*   I ate **a lot**.

Q 15   Write in French.

a He walks slowly.

_____

b He walks silently.

_____

c Fortunately he was there.

_____

d It was entirely his fault.

_____

_____

e He speaks politely.

_____

f He speaks quickly.

_____

g He drank too much.

_____

h He often spoke of his childhood.

_____

_____

16 Conjunctions

Conjunctions are words that join two parts of a sentence together. The most common one is **and**.

car **for (because)**

Point to watch

Do not confuse this with the preposition *pour*. If you wish to use the word **for** meaning **because**, remember to use *car*.

*Il a dû rentrer à la maison à pied **car** il avait perdu la clé de sa voiture.*
He had to walk home because he had lost his car key.
Car is an alternative to *parce que* **(because)**.

comme **as/like**

*Faites **comme** vous voulez.*   Do **as** you like.

donc **so** (reason)

Points to watch

Do not use this word at the beginning of a sentence, it introduces a clause.

*Il est malade, **donc** il est resté à la maison.*
He is ill, **so** he stayed at home.

lorsque, quand   when

*Je l'ai vu **quand** il est arrivé.*   I saw him **when** he arrived.

Point to watch

Be very careful when using **quand** and **lorsque.** The future tense is frequently needed in French after these two conjunctions where in English we use the present tense,

e.g.   *Je te téléphonerai **quand** je serai à Paris.*
I shall telephone you **when** I am in Paris (i.e. when I shall be in Paris).

---

parce que   because

*Il n'a pas réussi **parce qu**'il n'a pas travaillé.*
He didn't succeed **because** he didn't work.

Point to watch

There is no hyphenation between these two words.

puisque   since (reason) = **because**

*Il travaille dur **puisqu**'il désire réussir.*
He is working hard **since** (i.e. **because**) he wants to succeed.

pendant que   during, while

***Pendant qu**'il lisait son journal, on a sonné à la porte.*
While he was reading his newspaper someone rang the door-bell.

Q 16   Write in French.

a He went to bed because he was tired.

_____

_____

b He plays like his brother.

_____

_____

c He was tired so he went to bed.

_____

_____

d When he arrives, I shall tell him.

_____

_____

e He is sad because he has lost his money.

_____

_____

f While I was watching TV the burglars entered.

_____

_____

g I played tennis while Paul stayed in bed.

_____

_____

17 Prepositions

A preposition is a word placed before a noun or a pronoun to indicate time, place or condition, e.g. **near** the river.

Point to watch

One of the most important things to remember as far as prepositions are concerned is that frequently there is no one single word in French which will translate a particular word in English. **In** is a difficult word to translate, e.g. *dans*, *en*, *à*, etc. Usually only one of these will be appropriate in the particular circumstances. Below are some guidelines for the use of some everyday prepositions.

About

Point to watch

When translating **about** into French, you must first work out whether **about** means **approximately**, **concerning**, or **on the subject of**.

approximately
à peu près

> *J'ai à peu près cinquante livres.*   I have **about** fifty books.

environ

> *J'arriverai à dix heures environ.*   I shall arrive **about** ten o'clock.

vers   (similar to *environ*)

> *Nous partirons vers deux heures.*   We shall leave **about** two o'clock.

concerning
à propos de

> *Je voudrais vous parler à propos de votre visite.*
> I'd like to speak to you **about** your visit.

on the subject of
au sujet de (similar to *à propos de*)

> *Il parlait au sujet des vacances.*
> He was speaking **about** the holidays.

what
de quoi

> *De quoi parles-tu?*
> What are you talking **about**?

Along

Point to watch

The word for **along** could be either *le long de*, *dans* or *sur*.

le long de

> *Il marchait le long du quai.*   He was walking **along** the platform.

dans

> *Il marchait dans la rue.*   He was walking **along** the street.

sur

> *La voiture roulait vite sur la route.*
> The car was going quickly **along** the road.

Among(st)

parmi

> *Il a caché le trésor **parmi** les rochers.*
> He hid the treasure **among** the rocks.

entre

> *Nous étions **entre** amis.*   We were **among** friends.

Before

Point to watch

You need to work out whether **before** means **(a)** before in time, **(b)** already, or **(c)** in front of.

avant

> *Venez **avant** midi.*   Come **before** noon.

déjà   **already**

> *Je l'ai **déjà** vu.*   I've seen it **before**.

devant   **in front of**

> *Tenez-vous **devant** la classe.*   Stand **before** (in front of) the class.

By

Point to watch

There are five ways of translating **by**. Look at the examples.

à

> *Je viendrai **à** vélo.*   I'll come **by** bike.

de

> *La vieille dame descendait la rue, suivie **d'**un voleur.*
> The old lady went down the street, followed **by** a thief.

en

> *J'y suis allé **en** auto.*   I went there **by** car.

par

> *Les enfants ont été punis **par** leur mère.*
> The children have been punished **by** their mother.

près de   **near/by**

> *Asseyez-vous près du feu.*   Sit **by** the fire.

For

> ### Point to watch
>
> This can be translated by ***depuis*** (if the action is still going on),
> ***pendant*** (if the action has stopped), or ***pour*** (if the action is in the
> future).

To say 'I have been learning French **for** five years' you have to use the
French sentence *J'apprends le français **depuis** cinq ans* (literally: 'I learn
French since five years').

> ### Point to watch
>
> The implication is that I am still learning French.

To say 'He has been here for three days' you have use the French sentence
*Il est ici **depuis** trois jours* (literally 'He is here since three days').

To say 'He had been living in Paris for two years' you have to use the
French sentence *Il habitait Paris **depuis** deux ans* (literally 'He was living in
Paris since two years').

> ### Point to watch
>
> In the above examples, the perfect tense in English (I have been
> learning) has changed to a present tense in French (***j'apprends***) and
> the pluperfect tense in English (he had been living) has changed to an
> imperfect tense in French (***habitait***) (see page 106 on the imperfect
> tense).

pendant   **for** (during)

> *J'ai travaillé **pendant** trois heures.*   I worked **for** three hours.

> ### Point to watch
>
> In this example you are implying that you are no longer working.

pour   **for** (future or pre-arranged time)

> *Nous serons là **pour** trois semaines.*   We shall be there **for** three
> weeks.

In

Point to watch

In can be either *à, dans, de, en* or *sous*. Look at the examples.

à

*Les enfants sont **à** l'école.*   The children are **in** school.

à l'intérieur	**inside**	*au lit*	**in** bed
à Londres	**in** London	*au soleil*	**in** the sun
à la mode	**in** fashion	*à haute voix*	**in** a loud voice

dans

*Ils sont **dans** la salle à manger.*   They are **in** the dining-room.

de

*Elle s'habille **de** noir.*   She dresses **in** black.

en

*J'habite **en** France.*   I live **in** France.
*Vous y arriverez **en** quatre heures.*   You will get there **in** four hours.
*Elle s'habille **en** pantalon.*   She dresses **in** trousers.

sous

*J'aime marcher **sous** la pluie.*   I like walking **in** the rain.

On

Point to watch

On can be either *sur, dans, de, en, par* or it can be simply left out. Look at the examples below.

sur

***sur la table*   **on** the table

à

à droite	**on** the right
à gauche	**on** the left
à pied	**on** foot
*Nous allons à l'école **à pied**.*	We go to school **on** foot.
à son retour	**on** his/her return
A son retour, il est allé la voir.	**On** his return he went to see her.

dans

*Je l'ai rencontré **dans** l'autobus.*   I met him **on** the bus.

de

| *d'un côté* | **on** one side |
| *de l'autre côté* | **on** the other side |

en

| *en vacances* | **on** holiday |
| *en vente* | **on** sale |

par

par une belle journée d'été   **on** a fine summer's day

Elle est venue lundi.   She came **on** Monday.

Out

Point to watch

Out can be either *hors* or *par*.

hors

hors de danger	**out** of danger
hors de la maison	**out** of the house
hors d'haleine	**out** of breath
hors de vue	**out** of sight

par

*Elle regardait **par** la fenêtre.*   She was looking out of the window.

Since

depuis   (See also **for**.)

*Il n'a rien fait **depuis** son arrivée.*
He has done nothing **since** he arrived.

Until

Jusqu'à

*Nous y resterons **jusqu'à** minuit.*
We shall stay there **until** midnight.

Point to watch

To say **until tomorrow**, you say *à demain* (literally: **to** tomorrow).

up, down, in, out with a verb of motion

In sentences such as:

He ran **into** the house.   She ran **down** the street.

you have to say

*Il est **entré** dans la maison en courant.*
(literally: He **entered** the house running.)

*Elle a **descendu** la rue en courant.*
(literally: She **went down** the street running.)

Q 17   Write in French.

a   about twenty cars

_____

b   He phoned about your holidays.

_____

c   It will start about three o'clock.

_____

_____

d   He walked along the beach.

_____

_____

e   He gave out the money among his friends.

_____

_____

f   He left before the end of the meal.

_____

_____

g   I have already done it.

_____

_____

h I will be in front of the cinema.

_____

i He travelled by bike and by car.

_____

j The baker's is near the station.

_____

k I have been living here for five years.

_____

l I had been studying French for ten years.

_____

m I stayed there for an hour.

_____

n I will be in Spain for a week.

_____

o In Paris short skirts are in fashion.

_____

p When you arrive in France, you will be in the city centre in an hour.

_____

_____

q When he went back to France he drove on the left.

_____

_____

r He took his tie from a wardrobe.

_____

_____

s He was now out of danger.

_____

_____

t Through the window I saw the thief.

_____

_____

u The clock is over the door.

_____

_____

v more than ten

_____

w He has slept since ten o'clock.

_____

_____

x He slept until ten o'clock.

_____

_____

y He ran in.

_____

z He ran out.

_____

18 Personal pronouns

Pronouns are words that stand in place of a noun. Personal pronouns stand in place of a person, e.g. instead of saying **the man**, you could say **he**.

Subject pronouns

je	I
tu	you
il/elle/on	he/she/one
nous	we
vous	you
ils/elles	they

Direct object pronouns and Indirect object pronouns

You need to know the difference between a direct object pronoun and an indirect object pronoun. Look at these sentences:

He sent a letter to his friend.
He sent his friend a letter.

Both these sentences mean exactly the same thing.

The direct object is the person or thing that has an action done to it. In both sentences you can see that the thing that was actually sent was a letter not a friend. Hence the direct object is **a letter** and **his friend** is the indirect object. To find an indirect pronoun in English, look out for the word 'to'. It may be there (see the first sentence) or it may be understood (i.e. it may be hidden) (see the second sentence).

Direct object pronouns.

Il me voit.	He sees **me**.
Il te voit.	He sees **you**.
Il le voit.	He sees **him** (or **it**).
Il la voit.	He sees **her** (or **it**).
Il nous voit.	He sees **us**.
Il vous voit.	He sees **you**.
Il les voit.	He sees **them**.

Indirect object pronouns

Il me donne l'argent.	He gives **me** the money.
Il te donne l'argent.	He gives **you** the money.
Il lui donne l'argent.	He give **him/her** the money.
Il nous donne l'argent.	He gives **us** the money.
Il vous donne l'argent.	He gives **you** the money.
Il leur donne l'argent.	He gives **them** the money.

Note that what is given in these sentences is the money and not me, etc. Hence me, etc are indirect object pronouns.

Direct object and indirect object pronouns are the same except in the third persons singular and plural.

Me, te, le and **la** become **m'**, **t'**, **l'** and **l'** before a vowel,

e.g. *Il m'écoute.* He listens to **me**.

Where do these pronouns go in a sentence?

The normal order of pronouns in French is:

1	2	3	4	5		
me						
te	*le*					
(se)	*la*	*lui*				
nous	*les*	*leur*	*y*	*en*	+	verb
vous						
(se)						

> e.g. *Je **te le** donne.*   I give **it to you.**
> *Il **m'en** a parlé.*   He talked **to me about it.**
> *Nous **les y** enverrons.*   We'll send **them there.**

The object pronouns always keep to this order, except in affirmative commands. In affirmative commands:

a The object pronouns follow the verb and are joined to the verb by hyphens.

b The direct object pronoun always precedes the indirect object pronoun.

c *Me* becomes *moi*, and *te* becomes *toi*, except before *en* when they become *m'en* and *t'en*.

d *Y* means **there** and *en* means **of it, of them** or **some.**

> e.g. *Je **lui en** ai donné.*   Affirmative statement:
>   I have given **some to him.**
>
> *Je ne **lui en** ai pas donné.*   Negative statement:
>   I have not given **any to him.**
>
> *Donnez-**lui-en.***   Affirmative command:
>   Give **some to him.**
>
> *Ne **lui en** donnez pas.*   Negative command:
>   Don't give **any to him.**
>
> *Donnez-**les-moi.***   Affirmative command:
>   Give **them to me.**
>
> *Donnez-**m'en.***   Affirmative command:
>   Give **me some.**

Q 18 Write in French.

a He helps me. _____

b He helps you. _____

c He helps him. _____

d He helps her. _____

e He helps us. _____

f He helps you. _____

g He helps them. _____

h He writes to me. _____

i He writes to you. _____

j He writes to him. _____

k He writes to her. _____

l He writes to us. _____

m He writes to you. _____

n He writes to them. _____

o He gives it to him. _____

p Give it to him. _____

q They do not give them to them.

_____

r Do not give them to them. _____

s I saw him there. _____

t I have two of them. _____

19 Possessive pronouns

These are words which stand in place of a noun and indicate possession,
e.g. **mine, yours,** etc.

	singular		plural	
	masculine	feminine	masculine	feminine
mine	*le mien*	*la mienne*	*les miens*	*les miennes*
yours	*le tien*	*la tienne*	*les tiens*	*les tiennes*
his/hers	*le sien*	*la sienne*	*les siens*	*les siennes*
ours	*le nôtre*	*la nôtre*	*les nôtres*	*les nôtres*
yours	*le vôtre*	*la vôtre*	*les vôtres*	*les vôtres*
theirs	*le leur*	*la leur*	*les leurs*	*les leurs*

e.g. *Où est ton billet? Voici **le mien.***
Where is your ticket? Here is **mine.**

*Je n'ai pas de voiture. Pouvons-nous y aller dans **la vôtre?***
I haven't a car. Can we go there in **yours?**

In this last sentence **yours** = your car. Since **car** is feminine in French (*la voiture*), the feminine possessive pronoun must be used irrespective of the gender of the possessor.

Possession may also be expressed in the following way:
A qui est ce stylo? C'est à moi.   **Whose** pen is this? It's **mine.**

Q 19   **Write in French.**

a These books are mine and these pencils are yours.

_____

b This book is mine and this chair is yours.

_____

c The book is his and the car is his.

_____

d The book is hers and the car is hers.

_____

e The money is ours and the books are ours.

_____

f The chair is yours and the books are yours.

_____

g The house is theirs and the pens are theirs.

_____

---

20 Demonstrative pronouns

These pronouns are used to say **this one/that one**, and in the plural, **these ones/those ones**.

singular		plural	
masculine	feminine	masculine	feminine
celui	*celle*	*ceux*	*celles*

If you wish to stress **this/these** or **that/those**, then the endings *-ci* or *-là* respectively may be added,

e.g. *Voici deux livres.* **Celui-ci** *est à moi.* **Celui-là** *est à Natalie.*
Here are two books. **This one** (here) is mine. **That one** (there) is Natalie's.

Ces chaussures sont à 400F, mais **celles-là** *sont à 350F.*
These shoes cost 400F, but **those** cost 350F.

Always check carefully the gender of the pronouns you are using.

Ceci/cela   this/that
Ecoutez **ceci.**   Listen to **this.**
Qui a dit **cela?**   Who said **that?**

Cela is often shortened to *ça*:
Qui a dit **ça?**   Who said **that?**
Ça, *c'est vrai.*   **That's** true.

Q 20   Write in French.

a Here are some bags. The one on the left is blue.
The ones on the table are green. (*un sac*)

_____

_____

_____

b Here are some shirts. The one on the left is blue.
The ones on the table are green. (*une chemise*)

_____

_____

_____

c Here are some swimsuits. This one is blue and that one is
red. (*un maillot de bain*)

_____

_____

d Here are two jackets. This one is blue and that one is red.
(*une veste*)

_____

_____

e Here are some gloves. These are red and those are blue.
(*un gant*)

_____

_____

f Here are some sunglasses. These are red and those are
blue. (*des lunettes de soleil*)

_____

_____

g This is good and that is bad.

_____

_____

21 Disjunctive (or emphatic) pronouns

These are words that stand in place of a noun and emphasise which person you are talking about, e.g. **Me!**

moi	me/I	*nous*	us/we
toi	you	*vous*	you
lui	him/he	*eux*	them/they (masc.)
elle	her/she	*elles*	them/they (fem.)

Disjunctive pronouns should be used:

a After prepositions,

e.g. *devant **moi***   in front of **me**
*sans **eux***   without **them**
*chez **elle***   at **her** house

b To emphasise a pronoun at the beginning of a sentence,

e.g. ***Moi**, je l'ai fait*   **I** did it.
***Lui**, il est venu.*   **He** came.

c When a pronoun stands alone,

e.g. *Qui l'a fait? – **Moi**.*   Who did it? – **I did**.

d In comparisons,

e.g. *Vous êtes plus intelligent que **moi**.*
You are more intelligent than **me**.

*Il est aussi grand que **toi**.*   He is as tall as **you**.

e With *c'est* and *ce sont*,

e.g. *C'est **vous**.*   It's **you**.
*Ce sont **elles**.*   It's **them** (fem.).

Ce sont is used only with the third person plural.

Points to watch

The word *-même* may be added to the above words to translate **-self**,
   e.g.   *moi-même* my**self**, *toi-même* your**self**, etc.
Note also ***soi-même***, one**self**. Use this when you are using **on**,
   e.g.   *On peut le faire **soi-même**.* One can do it **oneself**.

Q 21   Write in French.

a The present is for me

_____

b The present is for you (sing.).

_____

c The present is for him.

_____

d The present is for her.

_____

e The present is for us.

_____

f The present is for you (pl.).

_____

g The present is for them (male).

_____

h The present is for them (female).

_____

i I did it myself.

_____

j She did it herself.

_____

k He did it, not me.

_____

l Who is guilty? You!

_____

m Who is guilty? I am.

_____

22 Relative pronouns

A relative pronoun is a word like **which, that, who, whom,** which links
one part of a sentence with another,

> e.g.   This is the dog **that** bit me.

a *qui*   **who, which** (subject)
 que   **whom, that** (object)
 dont   **whose, of whom, of which**

> e.g.   *Les enfants **qui** habitent à côté sont gentils.*
> The children **who** live next door are nice.
>
> *Les enfants **que** vous voyez sont méchants.*
> The children **who(m)** you see are nasty.
>
> *Voici le livre **dont** vous avez besoin.*
> Here is the book **which** you need.

b *ce qui*   **what**
 ce que   **what**
 ce dont   **what**

> e.g.   *Dites-moi **ce qui** est arrivé.*
> Tell me **what** has happened.
>
> *Dites-moi **ce que** vous avez fait.*
> Tell me **what** you did.
>
> *Dites-moi **ce dont** vous avez besoin.*
> Tell me **what** you need.

c *lequel* (masc.)
 laquelle (fem.)   } **(the...) which**
 lesquels (masc. pl.)
 lesquelles (fem. pl.)

Lequel, etc. may be used on their own as questions,

> e.g.   *J'ai rapporté un de vos livres. – **Lequel**?*
> I've brought back one of your books. – **Which** one?
>
> *Puis-je emprunter une de tes revues? – **Laquelle**?*
> May I borrow one of your magazines? – **Which** one?

Q 22 **Write in French.**

a The book that I read is on the table.

_____

_____

b The man that wrote the book is at the table.

_____

_____

c The book that he is talking about is on the table.

_____

_____

d I cannot remember what I saw.

_____

e I do not know what happened.

_____

f Here are some cakes. Which one do you want?
Which ones do you want?

_____

_____

g Here are some apples. Which one do you want?
Which ones do you want?

_____

_____

23 Six useful pronouns
autre **other**

*J'ai vendu quelques livres mais je garderai **les autres**.*
I have sold some books but I shall keep **the others**.

chacun(e) **each one**

*Regardez ces voitures. **Chacune** est rouillée.*
Look at those cars. **Each one** (every one of them) is rusty.

N'importe is a very useful pronoun:

n'importe qui   **anybody**

> *N'importe qui peut le faire.*   **Anybody** can do it.

n'importe quoi   **anything**

> *Rapportez n'importe quoi.*   Bring back **anything**.

n'importe quel(le)(s)   **any**

> *Vous le trouverez dans n'importe quelle épicerie.*
> You will find it at **any** grocer's.

plusieurs   **several**

> *As-tu des CDs? Oui, j'en ai plusieurs.*
> Have you any CDs? Yes, I have **several**.

quelqu'un   **someone**

> *Attendez-vous quelqu'un?*   Are you waiting for **someone**?

quelques-un(e)(s)   **some, a few**

> *Quelques-uns de vos élèves sont paresseux.*
> **Some** of your pupils are lazy.

tout   **everything**

> *Il connaît tout.*   He knows **everything**.

tout le monde   **everybody**

> *Tout le monde est arrivé.* **Everybody** has arrived.

Q 23   **Write in French.**

a   Where are the others?

_____

b   Each one is very expensive.

_____

c   She goes out with anybody.

_____

d   You can take anything.

_____

e You can go there any day.

_____

f I have been there several times.

_____

g There is someone downstairs.

_____

h Some of the plates were dirty.

_____

i Everything is normal.

_____

j Everybody went to the party.

_____

24 The present tense

How to recognise the present tense in English

The present tense is used to express what **happens**, perhaps regularly; what is **happening** now and what **does happen** (**does** is added to give emphasis). Some examples in English:

I **live** in Birmingham.   general statement
I **am living** in Birmingham.   true now
I **do live** in Birmingham.   emphatic, perhaps contradicting another speaker's: 'You don't live in Birmingham.'

Point to watch

All of the above forms would be translated into French by the one form: *J'habite Birmingham.* You must not translate **am**, or **do**, in the above sentences. The key idea is **live/living**.

Point to watch

As in English, the present tense in French can also be used to refer to something which is going to take place in the near future:

e.g. *Je joue au tennis demain.*   **I'm playing** tennis tomorrow.

How to form the present tense in French

All French verbs can be divided into two groups: those which are **regular**, and those which are **irregular**. The great majority are regular, which means that they follow a pattern. Once you know the pattern, you can generate any form. Irregular verbs sometimes differ only slightly, but others can be totally unique. You must, therefore, learn these separately.

Regular verbs

Regular verbs are divided into three groups, described by referring to the last two letters of the verb infinitive. They are described as:

-er (e.g. *habiter* **to** live; *travailler* **to** work; *aimer* **to** like, love)

-ir (e.g. *finir* **to** finish; *servir* **to** serve; *choisir* **to** choose)

or *-re* (e.g. *vendre* **to** sell; *perdre* **to** lose; *attendre* **to** wait)

Point to watch

The form of the verb which you will find quoted in a dictionary is the **infinitive**. E.g. if you look up, in an English-French, French-English dictionary,

buy you will find *acheter*
fill you will find *remplir*
reply you will find *répondre*

In English, we often use **to** before the infinitive, e.g. **to** buy; **to** fill and **to** reply. In the dictionary listing, however, **to** is always left out.

To form the present tense, remove the infinitive **ending** (you wouldn't say in English, **I to buy**, or **we to fill**!), this leaves you with the **stem**. Then add the correct 'person' ending. French has an ending for each person (I; you; he/she/it/one; we; they), so you <u>always</u> need to add an ending to the stem.

Type 1: *-er* verbs

Regular *-er* verbs

donner – **to** give
je donne I give
tu donnes you (sing.) give
il donne he/it gives
elle donne she/it gives
on donne one gives
nous donnons we give
vous donnez you (plural or polite singular form) give

| *ils donnent* | they give (masculine form or a mixed group of masculine and feminine) |
| *elles donnent* | they give (feminine form) |

You will see that the endings for type 1 regular verbs are:

-e, -es, -e, -e, -e, -ons, -ez, -ent, -ent.

Point to watch

il (**he** or **it**), *elle* (**she** or **it**), and *on* (**one**) always have the same endings, so, in the tables which follow, they will be listed together. Similarly, *ils* (**they,** masculine or a mixed group) and *elles* (**they,** feminine only) always have the same form, and will be listed together.

Point to watch

Remember to omit the *e* of *je* when it is followed by a vowel or *h,*

e.g. *j'habite, j'arrive*

Q 24.1   Write in French.

a She prepares the lunch. (*préparer*)

_____

b He is looking for the house. (*chercher*)

_____

c I eat cheese. (*manger*)

_____

d We live in Newcastle. (*habiter*)

_____

e They walk fast. (*marcher*)

_____

f You (plural) find English easy. (*trouver*)

_____

g I live on the coast. (*habiter*)

_____

> **h** You (sing.; formal) do sing well. (*chanter*)
>
> _____
>
> **i** We are watching television. (*regarder*)
>
> _____
>
> **j** (The film) It is starting at 8.00 pm. (*commencer*)
>
> _____

Irregular *-er* verbs

Point to watch

The stems of some verbs change slightly but they keep the same endings.

For example, the verb *manger* (**to eat**) has only one irregularity in the present tense, which is the addition of *e* in the *nous* form, i.e. *nous mangeons*. The *e* is added to keep the *g* sound soft.

Similarly, the verb *commencer* requires a cedilla (*ç*) in the *nous* form, to keep the *c* sound soft: *nous commençons*.

There are verbs whose stem changes are more irregular. You can check the most common of these at the back of this book.

Point to watch

It is worthwhile checking verbs you are not familiar with. If irreg. is quoted after the entry <u>in the French to English section</u> of a dictionary, then you should check the verb either in this book or at the back of the dictionary.

Point to watch

Aller (**to go**) is the most irregular *-er* verb:

*je **vais***	I go
*tu **vas***	you (sing.) go
*il/elle/on **va***	he/she it/one goes
*nous **allons***	we go
*vous **allez***	you (plural or formal sing.) go
*ils/elles **vont***	they go

Type 2: *-ir* verbs

Regular *-ir* verbs have the following endings added to the stem:

-is, -is, -it, -it, -it, -issons, -issez, -issent, -issent.

finir – **to** finish
je finis   *nous finissons*
tu finis   *vous finissez*
il/elle/on finit *ils/elles finissent*

Q 24 2 **Write in French.**

 a I choose the blue car. (*choisir*)

  _____

 b The children finish their homework. (*finir*)

  _____

 c You (sing.; informal) are filling the tank. (*remplir*)

  _____

 d We do choose the menu. (*choisir*)

  _____

 e They are building a garage. (*bâtir*)

  _____

Irregular *-ir* verbs

You will find the most useful irregular *-ir* verbs listed at the back of the book.

Point to watch

An important verb, *avoir* (**to have**), is irregular:

avoir - **to have**
j'ai   *nous avons*
tu as   *vous avez*
il/elle/on a *ils/elles ont*

Type 3: *-re* verbs

Regular *-re* verbs have the following endings added to the stem:

-s, -s, -, -, -, -ons, -ez, -ent, -ent.

vendre – **to** sell
je vends   *nous vend**ons***
tu vend**s**   *vous vend**ez***
il/elle/on vend   *ils/elles vend**ent***

Q 24.3   **Write in French.**

a I wait for the bus. (*attendre*)

_____

b Frédérique hears the dog. (*entendre*)

_____

c We return the books. (*rendre*)

_____

d They are losing the match. (*perdre*)

_____

e You (pl.) do sell ice-creams. (*vendre*)

_____

f She replies immediately. (*répondre*)

_____

g You (sing.; informal) do go down the stairs. (*descendre*)

_____

h I hang the washing out. (*pendre*)

_____

i She is selling the house. (*vendre*)

_____

j They give the money back. (*rendre*)

_____

Irregular *-re* verbs

Listed at the back of the book are some of the more common irregular *-re* verbs.

Point to watch

The verb *être* is the most irregular of *-re* verbs:

être – to be

je **suis**	nous **sommes**
tu **es**	vous **êtes**
il/elle/on **est**	ils/elles **sont**

Q 24.4 Write in French.

a He goes to Paris.

_____

b Anne has a cat.

_____

c Pierre is Belgian.

_____

d We are in Switzerland.

_____

e They have three children.

_____

f I'm going to town.

_____

g You (pl.) are going on holiday.

_____

h You (sing.; informal) do have time.

_____

i I have a cold.

_____

j Paul and Jeanne are in the garden.

Point to watch

In all regular verbs (*-er, -ir* and *re)*, and in the vast majority of irregular verbs too, the endings *-ons; -ez* and *-ent* are reliable:

-ons	→	nous *(*we form of verb)
-ez	→	vous (**you, plural** or **formal singular** form of verb)
-ent	→	ils/elles (**they** form of verb)

25 Two special constructions in the present tense: *VENIR DE* and *DEPUIS*

French uses a present tense verb in certain constructions where, in English, a perfect tense is used.

Venir de – To have just done something

Compare the English and French in these phrases:

Present tense verb	**Perfect tense verb**
*Je **viens de** recevoir ta lettre.*	I **have just** received your letter.
*Nous **venons** d'arriver.*	We **have just** arrived.

How to use venir de

Use the <u>present tense</u> of *venir*.

The action verb (**what** has just been done) must be in the <u>infinitive</u> (this ends in either *-er*, *-re*, or *-ir*) e.g. *manger, perdre, choisir.*

Point to watch

Venir is an irregular verb. Check its present tense forms before doing the following exercise.

Q 25.1   Write in French.

a   He has just written to his friend. (*écrire*)

_____

b   The students have just finished the exam. (*finir*)

_____

c The manager has just started the meeting. (*commencer*)

_____

_____

d My team has just won. (*gagner*)

_____

_____

e You (plural) have just missed the plane. (*manquer*)

_____

_____

Point to watch

Using the present tense of *venir* with *de* + **infinitive** translates **have** or **has (just done)**. If you want to express **had (just done)** see unit 35, p. 107.

Depuis – since/for (+ time phrase)

Compare the English and French in these phrases:

Present tense verb	Perfect tense verb
J'habite ici depuis un an.	I have lived here for a year.
Il apprend le français depuis 1997.	He has been learning French since 1997.
Nous attendons depuis vingt minutes.	We've been waiting for twenty minutes.

Points to watch

It is as though, in English, we look back and describe what **has happened** or **has been happening** ...

since (+ a point in the past, e.g. 2 p.m.; yesterday; last year; the 19th century)

or for (+ a period of time, e.g. 10 minutes; 3 hours; 6 months; 5 years)

whereas, in French, the fact that it is **still** happening <u>in the present</u> is most important, and therefore a present tense verb is needed.

How to use depuis

Use the <u>present tense</u> of the French verb where, in English, we use a perfect tense.

Q 25.2 Write in French.

a They have worked at the town hall for three years.
(*travailler*)

_____

_____

b She has been studying chemistry for six months. (*étudier*)

_____

_____

c We have been swimming since 10.00. (*nager*)

_____

_____

d He has been an actor since the age of twelve.
(*être*: irregular!)

_____

_____

e My brother has been looking for the book for half an hour. (*chercher*)

_____

_____

Points to watch

Using the present tense with *depuis* translates **have** or **has** (**done/ been doing**). If you want to express **had** (**done/ been doing**) see unit 35, p. 107.

26 Negatives

The most common negatives in English are **not, never/not ever, nothing/not anything** and **nobody/not anybody**. Look out also for the contracted form **n't**. Here is a list of negatives in French.

ne ... pas (**not**) *ne ... rien* (**nothing**)
ne ... point (**not at all**) *ne ... aucun*(e) (**not one, not any**)
ne ... jamais (**never**) *ne ... guère* (**scarcely**)
ne ... personne (**nobody/no-one**) *ne ... ni ... (ni ...)* (**neither ... nor**)
ne ... plus (**no more, no longer**) *ne ... nulle part* (**nowhere**)

Point to watch

ne ... que (**only**) is used in the same way as negatives.

The negative is usually 'wrapped around' the verb:

In the present tense:

Je ne joue pas au tennis. I don't play tennis.
Il ne regarde pas la télé. He isn't watching T.V./
  He doesn't watch T.V.
Nous n'allons jamais. We **never** go.

Q 26.1 Write in French.

a We don't listen to the radio. (*écouter*)

_____

b They never play football. (*jouer*)

_____

c She buys nothing. (*acheter*)

_____

d I never wash the car. (*laver*)

_____

e Marc hardly eats. (*manger*)

_____

f They only eat vegetarian dishes. (*manger*)

_____

g You (sing.; informal) wait for nobody. (*attendre*)

_____

h We are going nowhere. (*aller*)

_____

i They don't sell bread any more. (*vendre*)

_____

j You (pl.) don't hear any noise. (*entendre*)

_____

In compound tenses, e.g. the perfect tense, the negative is 'wrapped around' the <u>auxiliary</u> verb,

e.g. *Je n'ai pas joué au tennis.*   I didn't play tennis.
      Il n'a pas regardé la télévision.   He hasn't watched television.
      Nous ne sommes jamais allés.   We have **never** been.

Points to watch

ne ... personne is an exception. In compound tenses, it is 'wrapped around' the <u>whole</u> verb:

e.g. *Je n'ai vu personne.*   I saw **nobody**.

The following are also exceptions: *ne ... ni ... ni ...* ; *ne ... nulle part* and *aucun(e)*,

e.g. *Je n'ai pris ni la bière ni le cidre.*
      I had **neither** the beer **nor** the cider.

      Ils n'ont visité nulle part.
      They have visited **nowhere**.

      Nous n'avons vu aucune voiture.
      We didn't see **any** car.

Negatives with reflexive verbs

The reflexive pronoun stays immediately before the reflexive verb. The negative is 'wrapped around' it and the verb,

e.g. *Je ne me lève pas de bonne heure.*
      I don't get up early. (present tense)

      Je ne me suis pas levé de bonne heure.
      I didn't get up early. (perfect tense)

Similarly, with object pronouns,

e.g. *Je ne le vois pas.*   I don't (can't) see him (it).
      Je ne lui ai pas parlé.   I didn't speak to him (her).

Negatives with questions

Examples of question types iii, iv and v (see unit 28 on questions p. 71):

Est-ce que *Est-ce qu'ils ne vendent pas*
            de pain?   ⎫
Intonation *Ils ne vendent pas de pain?*   ⎬ Don't they sell bread?
Inversion *Ne vendent-ils pas de pain?*   ⎭

Points to watch

Certain negatives may be used as the subject of a sentence,

e.g. *Rien n'est arrivé.* **Nothing** has happened.
Personne n'a gagné. **Nobody** won.
Aucun avion n'a décollé. **No** plane took off.

Words like *rien, personne, jamais* and *nulle part* may be used on their own,

e.g. *Qu'a-t-il vu? Rien.* What did he see? **Nothing.**
Y êtes-vous allés? Jamais. Did you ever go there? **Never.**
Qui avez-vous vu? Personne. Who did you see? **Nobody.**
Où es-tu allé? Nulle part. Where did you go? **Nowhere.**

Combinations of negatives

a *Plus* before *rien*:
Ils ne font plus rien. They **no longer** do **anything.**

b *Jamais* before *rien*:
Ils ne nous donnent jamais rien. They **never** give us **anything.**

c *Plus* before *jamais*:
Nous ne mangerons plus jamais ici. We'll **never** eat here **ever again.**

d *Plus* before *personne*:
Je n'y rencontre plus personne. I don't meet **anyone** there **any more.**

e *Jamais* before *personne*:
Je n'y rencontre jamais personne. I **never** meet **anyone** there.

Points to watch

To remember the order of these combinations, remember these two sentences:

> *Je n'écouterai **plus jamais personne**.*
> I'll **never** listen to **anyone any more**.

and: *Je n'écouterai **plus jamais rien**.*
> I'll **never** listen to **anything any more**.

Negatives before an infinitive

Except for *ne ... personne*, both parts of the negative precede the infinitive <u>if the negative refers to that verb</u>:

*J'ai décidé de **ne jamais** revenir.*	I decided **never** to return. (never **returning**, rather than never **deciding**)
*J'ai décidé de **ne** voir **personne**.*	I decided to see **nobody**. (**seeing** nobody, not **deciding** nobody)

Points to watch

si = **yes** after a negative question or statement,

> e.g. *Vous ne l'avez pas vu? **Si**, je l'ai vu.*
> Haven't you seen it (him)? **Yes**, I have seen it (him).

Points to watch

Following a negative, *du, de la, de l'* and *des* become **de**:

*J'ai **des** pommes.*	→	*Je n'ai **pas de** pommes.*
I have **some** apples.	→	I haven't **any** apples.
*Nous prendrons **du** thé.*	→	*Nous ne prendrons **pas de** thé.*
We'll have **some** tea.	→	We'll not have **any** tea.

N'est-ce pas

This is a useful tag question (i.e. 'tagged' on the end of a sentence to check agreement or disagreement). It corresponds to a variety of negative tags in English, e.g. **haven't we?**; **didn't they?**; **wasn't he?**; **can't she?** etc.

e.g. *Nous avons réussi,* ***n'est ce pas?***   We succeeded, **didn't we?**
Ils ont gagné, ***n'est ce pas?***   They won, **didn't they?**
Il était malade, ***n'est ce pas?***   He was ill, **wasn't he?**
Elle peut venir, ***n'est ce pas?***   She can come, **can't she?**

Q 26.2 Write in French.

a They do not go to bed at 10 p.m. (*se coucher*)

_____

b She never cleans her teeth. (*se brosser*)

_____

c Their names aren't Jameau. (*s'appeler*: irregular!)

_____

d Who knows? No-one. (*savoir*: irregular!)

_____

e We never borrow anything. (*prêter*)

_____

f What is there on television? Nothing. (*il y a*)

_____

g Are you (sing.; informal) not playing the guitar? Yes! (*jouer de*)

_____

h I haven't got any free time. (*avoir*: irregular!)

_____

i It's Tuesday, isn't it? (*être*: irregular!)

_____

j My parents never worry. (*s'inquiéter*)

_____

Point to watch

In speech, the *ne* of the negative is often omitted. You must not write this though. Even French schoolchildren have this corrected in their work!

 e.g. you will hear:

   *Je joue **pas**.* = *Je **ne** joue **pas**.* I'm **not** playing.

   *Il parle **pas** anglais.* = *Il **ne** parle **pas** anglais.*
   He doesn't speak English.

27 Commands

How to recognise commands in English

Imperatives, or commands, are instructions to a person or people to **do** or **not do** something,

 e.g. Sit down. Don't sit down.
   Come here. Don't come here.

They can be suggestions, especially when directed at a group including the speaker,

 e.g. Let's go. Let's not go.
   Let's eat out. Let's not eat out.

How to form commands in French

In the case of *-re* and *-ir* verbs, use the present tense of the verb minus the subject pronoun:

	(*tu* form)	(*vous* form)		(*nous* form)	
attendre	*attends*	*attendez*	wait	*attendons*	let's wait
choisir	*choisis*	*choisissez*	choose	*choisissons*	let's choose

In the case of *-er* verbs, use the present tense of the verb, but drop the final *s* of the *tu* form. Remember to omit the subject pronoun:

	(*tu* form)	(*vous* form)		(*nous* form)	
regarder	*regarde*	*regardez*	look	*regardons*	let's look

Point to watch

Do not translate **let's**. Its meaning is contained in the command form in French.

Point to watch

Remember to check if a verb is irregular in the present tense. If it is, the command forms will also be irregular.

Negative commands

Wrap the *ne ... pas* (etc) around the verb:

(*tu* form)	*n'attends pas*	⎫ don't wait
(*vous* form)	*n'attendez pas*	⎬
(*nous* form)	*n'attendons pas*	⎭ let's **not** wait

(*tu* form)	*ne regarde pas*	⎫ don't look
(*vous* form)	*ne regardez pas*	⎬
(*nous* form)	*ne regardons pas*	⎭ let's **not** look

Commands with reflexive verbs (See also unit 29, p 75.)

Add the reflexive pronoun after the verb:

	(*tu* form)	(*vous* form)		(*nous* form)	
se lever	*lève-toi*	*levez-vous*	get up	*levons-nous*	let's get up

Point to watch

In this case, the reflexive pronoun *te* becomes *toi*, like a disjunctive pronoun.

When you give negative commands using reflexive verbs, wrap the *ne ... pas* (etc) around the verb. The reflexive pronoun comes before the verb:

(*tu* form)	*ne* te lève *pas*	⎫ don't get up
(*vous* form)	*ne* vous levez *pas*	⎬
(*nous* form)	*ne* nous levons *pas*	⎭ let's **not** get up

Points to watch

In negative commands, the reflexive pronoun is *te*, as normally.

Irregular command forms

Some common verbs have irregular command forms:

avoir	*aie*	*ayez*	*ayons*	**have**
être	*sois*	*soyez*	*soyons*	**be**
savoir	*sache*	*sachez*	*sachons*	**know**

e.g. **Soyez** *prudent!* **Be** careful!

Points to watch

The *tu* form of *aller*, when used to mean **go on!, go ahead!** is irregular: ***vas-y!***, but, from *s'en aller* to go away: ***va-t-en!* clear off!**

Q 27 **Write in French in all command forms (*tu; vous; nous*).**

a Listen!/Let's listen! (*écouter*)

_____

b Go to sleep!/Let's go to sleep!
(*dormir*: irregular in present tense!)

_____

_____

c Stop!/Let's stop! (*arrêter*)

_____

d Throw the ball!/Let's throw the ball! (*lancer*)

_____

_____

e Come on! (*venir*: irregular in present tense!)

_____

f Go to bed!/Let's go to bed! (*se coucher*)

_____

_____

g Don't get angry!/Let's not get angry! (*se fâcher*)

_____

_____

h Go!/Let's go! (*aller*)

_____

i Don't leave!/Let's not leave!
(*partir*: irregular in present tense!)

_____

j Sit down!/Let's sit down!
(*s'asseoir*: irregular in present tense!)

_____

28 Questions

There are **five** question types in French. All can be used in any tense.

i The most obvious is when a 'question word', or interrogative pronoun, is included,

> e.g. *Où habites-tu?*   **Where** do you live?
> *Qui est là?*   **Who** is there?

ii The tag question, *n'est-ce pas*, can be put on the end of a statement,

> e.g. *Il travaille ici, n'est-ce pas?*   He works here, **doesn't he**?
> *Nous dinerons, n'est-ce pas?*   We'll have dinner, **won't we**?
> *Ils ont fait de la voile, n'est-ce pas?*
> They went sailing, **didn't they**?

N'est-ce pas, as indicated in the examples above, can be used following a statement in any tense.

iii *Est-ce que* can be introduced at the beginning of <u>any</u> statement, in <u>any</u> tense,

> e.g. *Est-ce qu'il vient?*   Is he coming?
> *Est-ce qu'ils ont fait de la voile?*   Did they go sailing?
> *Est-ce que vous avez réservé?*   Have you booked?
> *Est-ce qu'il peut venir?*   Can he come?

iv Intonation can be used. By delivering any statement with a rising intonation at the end, this statement is converted into a question:

> *Il vient?*   Is he coming?
> *Nous dinerons?*   Shall we have dinner?
> *Vous avez réservé?*   Have you booked?

v The verb and its subject can be inverted, (their order becomes reversed normal statement order):

> *Il voit la photo.*   He sees the photo. (normal statement order)
> *Voit-il la photo?*   Does he see the photo? (inversion)

In questions where there is a compound verb or more than one verb, it is the <u>auxiliary</u> verb which is inverted,

> e.g. with compound verbs:
> *Vous avez réservé*   You have booked.
> (normal statement order)
> *Avez-vous réservé?*   Have you booked? (inversion)

> e.g. with a main verb + infinitive:
> *Il peut venir*   He can come. (normal statement order)
> *Peut-il venir?*   Can he come? (inversion)

Point to watch

In inverted questions, if the subject is a pronoun, remember to hyphenate the verb and the pronoun.

Point to watch

To preserve the 'pronunciation flow', you may need to introduce a *-t-* between the inverted verb and its subject,

     e.g. *A-t-il des frères?*   Does he have any brothers?

This *-t-* has no meaning, it simply aids pronunciation.

Or if using a noun, you will need to introduce a pronoun, and invert this and the verb,

     e.g. *Votre frère, est-il à la maison?*   Is your brother at home?
            Antoine, est-il arrivé?   Has Antoine arrived?

Point to watch

The inverted question-type is not usually used in the first person singular (*je*) forms. Two exceptions are *puis-je* and *pourrais-je*:

Puis-je vous aider?   Can I help you?
Pourrais-je parler avec M. Cressot?
Could I speak to Mr. Cressot?

Point to watch

N'est-ce pas is rather old-fashioned and is not often used in speech. Question-types **iv** and **v** are <u>very</u> common in speech, much more than the inversion type.

Question words (interrogative pronouns)

a *Combien?* (+ verb)   **How much?/How many?**
   Combien as-tu gagné?   **How much** did you earn (win)?
   Combien ont joué?   **How many** played?

   Combien de ...? (+ noun)   **How much?/How many?**
   Combien d'argent as-tu?   **How much** money do you have?
   Combien de personnes   **How many** people have arrived?
    sont arrivées?

b *Comment?*
  Comment vas-tu?
  Comment ça s'écrit?

How?
How are you?
How do you spell it?

c *Où?*
  Où habitez-vous?

Where?
Where do you live?

d *D'où*
  D'où êtes-vous?

Where from?
Where are you from?

e *Pourquoi?*
  Pourquoi es-tu venu?

Why?
Why did you come?

f *Quand?*
  Quand est-ce que tu rentres?

When?
When are you going back (home)?

g *Que?*
  Qu'est ce que?
  Qu'as-tu vu?
  Qu'est-ce que tu as vu?

What? (as the object)

} **What** have you seen?

h *Qui?*
  Qui est-ce qui?

Who? (as the <u>subject</u> of the question)

  Qui a dit cela?
  Qui est-ce qui a dit cela?

} **Who** said that?

i *Qui?*
  Qui est-ce que?

Whom? (as the <u>object</u> of the sentence)

  Qui as-tu vu?
  Qui est-ce que tu as vu?

} **Whom** did you see?

j *Qu'est-ce qui?*
  Qu'est-ce qui est arrivé?

What? (as the subject)
What has happened?

k The following are adjectives and must agree with the noun to which they refer:

  Quel (masc.) + noun
  Quelle (fem.) + noun
  Quels (masc. pl.) + noun
  Quelles (fem. pl.) + noun

} **What? Which?**

  Quels livres?
  Quelle maison?

What (Which) books?
What (Which) house?

Point to watch

With the exception of *qui*, when used as <u>the subject</u> of the sentence (see **h** above), these 'question words' are most commonly followed by a question of the **inversion-** or **est-ce-que-** type. Questions such as:

> *Tu habites-où?*   **Where** do you live?
> *Tu viens quand?*   **When** are you coming?

do occur, but they tend to be used in speech rather than written. An exception is:

> *C'est combien?*   **How much** is it?

Q 28   **Write in French.**

    a   Who lives here? (*habiter*)

    _____

    b   Where do you (sing.; informal) work? (*travailler*)

    _____

    _____

    c   When do you (pl.) go on holiday? (*aller*: irregular!)

    _____

    _____

    d   Why are they in Paris? (*être*: irregular!)

    _____

    _____

    e   Where is the train coming from? (*venir:* irregular!)

    _____

    _____

    f   Do you (sing.; informal) study Spanish? (*étudier*)

    _____

    _____

    g   Do you (plural) have to leave now? (*devoir:* irregular!)

    _____

    _____

h Do they have a computer? (*avoir*: irregular!)

_____

_____

i Is she staying at the hotel? (*rester*)

_____

_____

j Do we want to take part? (*vouloir*: irregular!)

_____

_____

29 Reflexive verbs

How to recognise a reflexive verb in English

A reflexive verb tends to describe an action being done to **oneself**, or to **each other**:

to wash	→ to wash the car	(**not** reflexive)
	→ to wash oneself	(reflexive)
to write	→ to write a letter	(**not** reflexive)
	→ to write to each other	(reflexive)

It is formed just like any other verb in a particular tense. There are regular and irregular reflexive verbs.

In French, reflexive verbs always have an extra pronoun, called a reflexive pronoun, preceding the verb. These pronouns are:

(*je*)	*me*
(*tu*)	*te*
(*il/elle/on*)	*se*
(*nous*)	*nous*
(*vous*)	*vous*
(*ils/elles*)	*se*

e.g. in the present tense:
se laver – **to** wash (**oneself**)

*je **me** lave*	I wash (**myself**)
*tu **te** laves*	you (sing.) wash (**yourself**)
*il/elle/on **se** lave*	he/she/it/one washes (**himself/herself/itself/oneself**)
*nous **nous** lavons*	we wash (**ourselves**)
*vous **vous** lavez*	you (pl. or polite sing.) wash (**yourself**)
*ils/elles **se** lavent*	they wash (**themselves**)

Point to watch

In English the reflexive pronoun is often not used. In the above example, we would just say **I wash**, or **I get washed**. It is understood that the action is being done **to oneself**. In French you **must** use the correct reflexive pronoun each time, or the sentence is incomplete.

Questions

Examples of question types **iii**, **iv** and **v** (see unit 28):

Est-ce que	*Est-ce qu'elle se brosse les dents?*	⎫
Intonation	*Elle se brosse les dents?*	⎬ Does she brush her teeth?
Inversion	*Se brosse-t-elle les dents?*	⎭

Negatives

Remember that the reflexive pronoun goes immediately before the verb,

e.g. *Il **ne** se rase **pas**.*   He doesn't shave.
*Elle **ne** se couche **jamais** à minuit.*
She **never** goes to bed at midnight.

The reflexive pronoun goes immediately before the verb to which it refers. Be careful if you have more than one verb in the phrase,

e.g. *Tu peux **te** coucher.*   You can go to bed.
*Nous devons **nous** écrire.*   We must write to **each other**.

Point to watch

Be careful to match the reflexive pronoun with the subject of the verb (i.e. if the subject is *je*, you must use *me;* if the subject is *tu*, you must use *te*), even, as in the above examples, when the reflexive verb is in the infinitve.

Point to watch

In French, the reflexive pronoun is used when referring to parts of the body, where English would use a possessive adjective,

e.g. *Il **se** coupe la main.*   He cuts **his** hand.
*Nous **nous** lavons les cheveux.*   We are washing **our** hair.
*Je **me** brosse les dents.*   I brush **my** teeth.

Q 29 Write in French.

a My name is Giraud. (*s'appeler*: irregular!)

_____

b We are resting. (*se reposer*)

_____

c Virginie never relaxes. (*se détendre*)

_____

d You (sing.; informal) do your hair. (*se coiffer*)

_____

_____

e Do you (pl.) walk by the sea? (*se promener*)

_____

_____

f I wonder. (*se demander*)

_____

g They are going to bathe in the sea.
(*aller*: irregular!, *se baigner*)

_____

_____

h We must get up. (*devoir*: irregular!, *se lever*)

_____

i You (sing.; informal) must wake up at 7.00.
(*devoir*: irregular!, *se réveiller*)

_____

_____

j You (pl.) shave quickly. (*se raser*)

_____

30 The future tense

How to recognise the future tense in English

The future tense is used to express what **will** happen in the future:
e.g. in two minutes from now, tomorrow or next year. Look out for the
words **shall, will** or the abbreviations of these words in **I'll, we'll**, and the
negative forms **won't, shan't**, etc. Here are some examples in English:

> I **shall** go.
> He **will** stay.
> **We'll** do the work.
> He **won't** like it!
> I **shan't** forget it.

How to form the future tense in French

For most verbs, the stem to use is the <u>infinitive</u> of the verb.

Every verb, regular or irregular, uses the same endings. These endings are:

(je)	**-ai**
(tu)	**-as**
(il/elle/on)	**-a**
(nous)	**-ons**
(vous)	**-ez**
(ils/elles)	**-ont**

e.g. **infinitive** + **ending**

Je	*manger*	+ *ai*	⇒	*Je **mangerai*** (*le sandwich*).
				I **will eat** the sandwich.
Tu	*regarder*	+ *as*	⇒	*Tu **regarderas*** (*la télévision*).
				You'**ll watch** T.V.
Nous	*servir*	+ *ons*	⇒	*Nous **servirons*** (*le café*).
				We'**ll serve** coffee.
Vous	*attendr(e)*	+ *ez*	⇒	*Vous attendrez* (*le car*).
				You'**ll wait** for the coach.

> ### Point to watch
>
> Where have you seen these endings before? Some are identical to the
> present tense forms of *avoir* (**to have**). This may help you to
> remember them.

> ### Point to watch
>
> Look at the last ending, *-ont*. It is very like the present tense ending
> *-ent*. Be careful!

Look at these examples:

-er verbs: *donner*		-ir verbs: *finir*	
je donnerai	I **will** give	*je finirai*	I **will** finish
tu donneras	you **will** give	*tu finiras*	you **will** finish
il/elle/on donnera	he/she/it/one **will** give	*il/elle/on finira*	he/she/it/one **will** finish
nous donnerons	we **will** give	*nous finirons*	we **will** finish
vous donnerez	you **will** give	*vous finirez*	you **will** finish
ils/elles donneront	they **will** give	*ils/elles finiront*	they **will** finish

-re verbs: *vendre*	
je vendrai	I **will** sell
tu vendras	you **will** sell
il/elle/on vendra	he/she/it/one **will** sell
nous vendrons	we **will** sell
vous vendrez	you **will** sell
ils/elles vendront	they **will** sell

Point to watch

With -re verbs, drop the last -e of the infinitive before adding the ending.

Reflexive verbs

With reflexive verbs, remember to include the correct reflexive pronoun (see unit 29),

e.g. *se laver* (to get washed) → *Je me laverai*
I shall get washed.

se raser (to shave) → *Il se rasera* He'll shave.

se dépêcher (to hurry) → *Nous nous dépêcherons*
We'll hurry up.

Questions

Examples of question types iii, iv and v (see unit 28):

Est-ce que	*Est-ce qu'il demandera?*	
Intonation	*Il demandera?*	} Will he ask?
Inversion	*Demandera-t-il?*	

The negative

To form the negative: wrap the **ne ... pas** (etc) around the verb,

e.g. *Je ne vendrai pas.* — I will **not** sell.
Elles ne partiront jamais d'ici. — They will **never** leave here.
Il ne s'amusera pas chez Martin.
He won't enjoy himself at Martin's house.

Q 30.1 **Write in French.**

a I'll watch TV. (*regarder*)

_____

b He will not play. (*jouer*)

_____

c We'll carry the bag. (*porter*)

_____

d They will try. (*essayer*)

_____

e I shall go out tonight. (*sortir*)

_____

_____

f The train will leave at 10.05. (*partir*)

_____

_____

g She will stay at home. (*rester*)

_____

_____

h They will not wait for the bus. (*attendre*)

_____

_____

i You (sing.; informal) will lose your money. (*perdre*)

_____

_____

j I shan't remember. (*se rappeler*)

_____

_____

Irregular forms

Some verbs have an irregular stem (instead of using the infinitive). However, remember that the endings are the same for all verbs. Here is a list of the most useful irregular forms:

acheter	→	**j'achèterai**	falloir	→	**il faudra**
aller	→	**j'irai**	pleuvoir	→	**il pleuvra**
avoir	→	**j'aurai**	pouvoir	→	**je pourrai**
courir	→	**je courrai**	recevoir	→	**je recevrai**
devoir	→	**je devrai**	savoir	→	**je saurai**
envoyer	→	**j'enverrai**	venir	→	**je viendrai**
être	→	**je serai**	voir	→	**je verrai**
faire	→	**je ferai**	vouloir	→	**je voudrai**

Points to watch

Remember that **compounds** of these verbs will behave in the same way.

e.g.	*venir*	→	*je **viendrai***
but also	*devenir*	→	*je **deviendrai***
and	*se souvenir*	→	*je me **souviendrai***

You can check for other irregular forms in the tables at the back of the book.

Q 30.2 **Write in French.**

a I'll be in Paris next week. (*être*)

_____

b You (sing.; informal) won't see the film. (*voir*)

_____

c Will they want the tickets? (*vouloir*)

_____

d We shall go on Friday. (*aller*)

_____

_____

e Dad will do the washing up. (*faire*)

_____

_____

f She'll know tomorrow. (*savoir*)

_____

_____

g They will send the fax. (*envoyer*)

_____

_____

h We will receive the fax this afternoon. (*recevoir*)

_____

_____

i Pierre will not have enough time. (*avoir*)

_____

_____

j Will you (pl.) be able to help? (*pouvoir*, *aider*)

_____

_____

k It will rain this weekend. (*pleuvoir*)

_____

_____

l Will we have to book a table? (*falloir*, *réserver*)

_____

_____

Point to watch

Sometimes French uses the future to refer to future time, where, in English, we use a present tense. Look at these sentences:

*Quand elle **arrivera**, elle **mangera**.* (both verbs in the future)

When she arrives, she will eat. (one verb **in the present**, one in the future)

*Il **expliquera** quand il **viendra**.* (both verbs in the future)

He will explain **when he comes**. (one verb **in the present**, one in the future)

Use the future tense in both parts of the sentence in French, if both parts refer to future time. Identify such words as ***quand, lorsque*** (when), ***aussitôt que*** (as soon as) and ***dès que*** (as soon as) as the 'triggers' for this.

Q 30.3   **Write in French.**

a When I phone, I'll leave a message. (*téléphoner, laisser*)

_____

_____

b We'll send a postcard when we are in France. (*envoyer, être*: irregular!)

_____

_____

c As soon as they have the details, they will book. (*avoir*: irregular!, *réserver*)

_____

_____

d She will start work once she receives the contract. (*commencer, recevoir*: irregular!)

_____

_____

31 The future without the future tense

In both English and French you can use **going to (do)** to refer to something which will happen in the near future.

Use the correct present tense form of *aller* to match the subject of your sentence. The second verb is always in the infinitive,

e.g.   *aller* + **infinitive**

Je	*vais*	*écrire (une lettre).*	**I'm going to** write a letter.
Nous	*allons*	*manger (sur la terrasse).*	**We're going to** eat on the patio.
Ils	*vont*	*acheter (la voiture).*	They **are going to** buy the car.
Il	*va*	*voir (le match dimanche).*	He **is going to** see the match on Sunday.

Reflexive verbs

Remember to include the correct reflexive pronoun (see unit 29). This will always go immediately in front of the infinitive:

e.g.   *Je vais **me** reposer.*   I'm going to rest.
*Vous allez **vous** baigner?*   Are you going to bathe?
*Ils ne vont pas **se** voir.*   They are not going to see **each other**.

Questions

The form of *aller* is the main verb, so invert this and its subject in inversion-type questions. Examples of question types **iii**, **iv** and **v** (see unit 28):

Est-ce que	*Est-ce qu'ils **vont** acheter la voiture?*
Intonation	*Ils **vont** acheter la voiture?*
Inversion	***Vont-ils** acheter la voiture?*

Are they going to buy the car?

The negative

The form of *aller* is the main verb, so generally wrap the negative around this (but see unit 26 on certain negatives),

e.g.   *Je **ne** vais **rien** écrire.*   I'm **not** going to write **anything**.

*Nous n'allons **pas** manger en ville.*
We're **not** going to eat in town.

*Ils **ne** vont **jamais** acheter la voiture.*
They are **never** going to buy the car.

but: *Ils **ne** vont visiter **aucun** château.*
They are **not** going to visit **any** castles.

Point to watch

Aller is irregular. You need to learn it by heart.

Q 31 Write in French.

a We are going to ask. (*aller, demander*)

_____

_____

b They are going to take part. (*aller, participer*)

_____

_____

c You (sing.; informal) are not going to visit the cathedral.
(*aller, visiter*)

_____

_____

d They are not going to finish their homework today.
(*aller, finir*)

_____

_____

e She is going to send a fax. (*aller, envoyer*)

_____

_____

f Is he going to speak to M. Lombard? (*aller, parler*)

_____

_____

g Are we going to look for the key? (*aller, chercher*)

_____

_____

h I'm going to work in a bank. (*aller, travailler*)

_____

_____

i She is going to lie down. (*aller, se coucher*)

_____

_____

j We are going to get washed. (*aller, se laver*)

_____

_____

32 The conditional

How to recognise the conditional in English

The conditional is used to express what **would** or **should** happen. Look out for the abbreviations, as in **she'd**; **they'd**. Here are some examples in English:

> You **would** leave immediately.
> She'**d** like to work there.
> We **would** visit the castle.
> They **wouldn't** come if we said that.

How to form the conditional in French

Use the <u>same stem</u> as to form the future tense (for most verbs, this is the infinitive, but some verbs have an irregular stem, see page 81). Every verb, regular or irregular, uses the same endings. These are:

(*je*)	*-ais*
(*tu*)	*-ais*
(*il/elle/on*)	*-ait*
(*nous*)	*-ions*
(*vous*)	*-iez*
(*ils/elles*)	*-aient*

e.g. **infinitive + ending**

Je	*parler*	*ais*	→	*Je **parlerais** avec Henri.*
				I'**d talk** to Henri.
Tu	*partir*	*ais*	→	*Tu **partirais** tout de suite.*
				You'**d leave** immediately.
Ils	*perdr(e)*	*aient*	→	*Ils **perdraient** le match.*
				They **would lose** the match.
Nous	*visiter*	*ions*	→	*Nous **visiterions** le château.*
				We'**d visit** the castle.

Point to watch

You may recognise these endings as the **imperfect tense** endings.
It may help you to remember that:

> future stem + imperfect endings = conditional.

Point to watch

With *-re* verbs remove the last *-e* of the infinitive before adding the
ending.

Reflexive verbs

With reflexive verbs, remember to include the correct reflexive pronoun
(see unit 29),

> e.g. *Je **me baignerais** dans la mer.*
> I **would bathe** in the sea.
>
> *Nous **nous mettrions** en route très tôt.* We'**d set off** very early.
> *Je **me rappellerais** la date.* I'**d remember** the date.

Questions

Examples of question types **iii**, **iv** and **v** (see unit 28):

Est-ce que	*Est-ce que tu demanderais?*	
Intonation	*Tu demanderais?*	**Would** you ask?
Inversion	*Demanderais-tu?*	

The negative

To form the negative, wrap the *ne ... pas* (etc) around the verb,

> e.g. *Je **ne** vendrais **pas**.* I would **not** sell.
> *Elles **ne** partiraient **jamais** d'ici.*
> They would **never** leave here.

Q 32.1 Write in French.

 a I would work hard. (*travailler*)

 _____

 b We would swim in the afternoon. (*nager*)

 _____

 _____

c Helen would play tennis. (*jouer*)

_____

_____

d Jean and Claudie would visit their parents.
(*rendre visite à*)

_____

_____

e You (pl.) would find the village easily. (*trouver*)

_____

_____

f He would give the present to Michel. (*donner*)

_____

_____

g They would remember. (*se souvenir*)

_____

_____

h I would not learn a lot. (*apprendre*)

_____

_____

Q 32.2 **Write in French.**

a They would come. (*venir*: irregular!)

_____

b He would have to understand our problem. (*devoir*:
irregular!, *comprendre*)

_____

_____

c We would go straight to the coast. (*aller*: irregular!)

_____

_____

d Béatrice would know the answer. (*savoir*: irregular!)

_____

_____

e I would like to travel. (*vouloir*: irregular!, *voyager*)

_____

_____

f You (sing.; informal) would be able to try the trousers on.
(*pouvoir*: irregular!, *essayer*)

_____

_____

g The company would send the details. (*envoyer*: irregular!)

_____

_____

h You (pl.) would have some free time. (*avoir*: irregular!)

_____

_____

i My aunt and uncle would not be there. (*être*: irregular!)

_____

_____

j She would do it. (*faire*: irregular!)

_____

_____

Point to watch

If you can replace **would** with **used to** in English, <u>without changing the meaning</u>, then you need to use the imperfect tense, not the conditional,

e.g. We **would** go swimming every Saturday morning. =
We **used to** go swimming every Saturday morning. =
Imperfect tense

I **would** catch the 8.20 bus to go to school when we lived in Derby. = I **used to** catch the 8.20 bus. = Imperfect tense

Point to watch

If **could** can be replaced by **would be able** <u>without changing the meaning</u>, then you need to use the conditional. However, if **could** can be replaced by **was able to**, and therefore refers to the past, then you must use a past tense (see units 33 and 34),

> e.g. He **could** do it tomorrow. = He **would be able** to do it tomorrow. = Conditional

> but: He **could** swim last year. = He **was able to** swim last year. = Imperfect tense

33 The perfect tense

How to recognise the perfect tense in English

The perfect tense is used in English to express what **has happened** or **has been happening** in the past. Look out also for the contracted forms. Here are some examples:

I **have watched** T.V.   (contracted form: **I've watched** T.V.)
We **have been** working.   (contracted form: **We've been** working.)
They **have studied** hard. (contracted form: **They've studied** hard.)
It **has been** raining.   (contracted form: **It's been** raining.)

The perfect tense is made up of two parts, the present tense of the auxiliary verb + the past participle. You can see the pattern in these English sentences:

	auxiliary	past participle
I	have	watched.
You	have	listened.
He	has	eaten.

The auxiliary verb is **have/has**.

The past participle often ends in **-ed**, but can also end in **-n** (e.g. **taken; eaten; seen**) or in **-t** (e.g. **caught; bought; fought**).

Point to watch

The perfect tense in French is used to express what **has happened** or **has been happening**, but also what **happened** or **did happen** in the past. French, then, has one way only of saying:

> I **have watched** T.V./I **have been watching** T.V./I **watched** T.V./I **did watch** T.V. = *J'ai regardé la télé*;

90

and, similarly, one phase for:

It **has rained.**/It **has been raining.**/It **rained.**/It **did rain.** =
Il a plu.

Point to watch

The key idea is that the action has finished. If the action has not been completed (e.g. He has lived here for five years – **and <u>still</u> lives here**), then you need to use a different construction in French (see unit 25, p. 65).

Point to watch

If you want to say that an action has **just** occurred, you need to use a different construction in French (see unit 25, p. 60).

How to form the perfect tense in French

Just as in English, the perfect tense is made up of two parts, the present tense of the auxiliary verb and the past participle.

To form the past participle:

-*er* verbs: ⇢ remove *er*, add *é* ⇢ *manger* ⇢ *mangé*
-*ir* verbs: ⇢ remove *ir*, add *i* ⇢ *finir* ⇢ *fini*
-*re* verbs: ⇢ remove *re*, add *u* ⇢ *vendre* ⇢ *vendu*

The auxiliary verb to use is: *avoir* for the great majority of verbs
        être for a small group of verbs
        être for all reflexive verbs.

The perfect tense with *avoir*:

-*er* verbs: *donner*
j'ai donné
   I **have given**, I **gave**
tu as donné
il/elle/on a donné
nous avons donné
vous avez donné
ils/elles ont donné

-*ir* verbs: *finir*
j'ai fini
   I **have finished**, I **finished**
tu as fini
il/elle/on a fini
nous avons fini
vous avez fini
ils/elles ont fini

-re verbs: *vendre*
j'ai vendu   I **have sold**, I **sold**
tu as vendu
il/elle/on a vendu
nous avons vendu
vous avez vendu
ils/elles ont vendu

Point to watch

The past participle is identical for **all** persons of the verb (**I**; **you**; **we**; **he/she/it**; **they**). Only the auxiliary verb changes when you change person.

Questions

Examples of question types **iii**, **iv** and **v** (see unit 28):

Est-ce que	*Est-ce qu'il **a mangé?***	
Intonation	*Il **a mangé**?*	**Has** he **eaten**?/**Did** he **eat**?
Inversion	*A-t-il mangé?* *	

*NB The auxiliary verb only is inverted.

The negative

Wrap ***ne...pas*** (etc) around the auxiliary verb,

e.g.   *Je n'ai **pas** écouté les informations.*
I **haven't** listened/**didn't** listen to the news.

*Nous n'avons **pas** vendu la maison.*
We **haven't** sold/**didn't** sell the house.

*Ils n'ont **pas** servi le déjeuner.*
They **haven't** served/**didn't** serve lunch.

Q 33.1   Write in French.

a   She spent £100. (*dépenser*)

_____

_____

b   You (sing.; formal) have worked hard. (*travailler*)

_____

_____

c They've chosen the present. (*choisir*)

_____

_____

d Did they fill the case? (*remplir*)

_____

_____

e He has lost his passport. (*perdre*)

_____

_____

f I answered the question. (*répondre*)

_____

_____

g We heard nothing. (*entendre*)

_____

_____

h Have you (sing.; formal) tried the snails? (*déguster*)

_____

_____

i I waited half an hour for the bus. (*attendre*)

_____

_____

j We didn't spend much time on the beach. (*passer*)

_____

_____

Point to watch

There is a large number of irregular past participles. You must learn the most useful of these (see below).

Irregular perfect tense verbs formed with *avoir*

avoir	j'ai **eu**	I had, I have had
boire	j'ai **bu**	I drank, I have drunk
conduire	j'ai **conduit**	I drove, I have driven
connaître	j'ai **connu**	I knew, I have known
courir	j'ai **couru**	I ran, I have run
craindre	j'ai **craint**	I feared, I have feared
croire	j'ai **cru**	I believed, I have believed
devoir	j'ai **dû**	I had to/owed, I have had to/have owed
dire	j'ai **dit**	I said, I have said
écrire	j'ai **écrit**	I wrote, I have written
être	j'ai **été**	I have been, I was
faire	j'ai **fait**	I made, I did etc
falloir	il a **fallu**	It has been necessary, it was necessary
lire	j'ai **lu**	I read, I have read
mettre	j'ai **mis**	I put, I have put
ouvrir	j'ai **ouvert**	I opened, I have opened
pleuvoir	il a **plu**	it rained, it has rained
pouvoir	j'ai **pu**	I have been able, I was able
prendre	j'ai **pris**	I took, I have taken
recevoir	j'ai **reçu**	I received, I have received
rire	j'ai **ri**	I laughed, I have laughed
savoir	j'ai **su**	I knew, I have known
suivre	j'ai **suivi**	I followed, I have followed
vivre	j'ai **vécu**	I lived, I have lived
voir	j'ai **vu**	I saw, I have seen
vouloir	j'ai **voulu**	I wanted, I have wanted

Q 33.2   **Write in French.**

a M. Maillac read the newspaper. (*lire*)

_____

_____

b The children washed up. (*faire*)

_____

_____

c We have not received the letter. (*recevoir*)

_____

_____

d Did you (pl.) have a coffee? (*prendre*)

_____

_____

e My dad drove to the coast. (*conduire*)

_____

_____

f We drank champagne at the wedding. (*boire*)

_____

_____

g She didn't have flu. (*avoir*)

_____

_____

h I've been to the doctor's. (*être*)

_____

_____

i Have you (sing.; informal) seen the film? (*voir*)

_____

_____

j I set the table. (*mettre*)

_____

_____

Preceding direct object agreement

When the direct object appears before the *avoir* part of a verb in the perfect tense, the past participle must agree with that direct object. The agreement is the same as adjectival agreement:

To agree with a masculine direct object before the verb: add **nothing**.
To agree with a feminine direct object before the verb: add **e**.
To agree with a masculine plural direct object before the verb: add **s**.
To agree with a feminine plural direct object before the verb: add **es**.

The direct object may be a pronoun,

e.g. (*J'ai vu la fille.*)	(I saw the girl.)
Je l'ai vue.	I saw **her**.
	(feminine agreement)
(*Il a bu deux cafés.*)	(He drank two coffees.)
*Il **les** a bus.*	He drank **them**.
	(masculine plural agreement)
(*Elle a envoyé les lettres.*)	(She's sent the letters.)
*Elle **les** a envoyées.*	She's sent **them**.
	(feminine plural agreement)

The direct object may be a noun,

e.g. *Voilà **les livres** que j'ai lus.*
Here are **the books** (which) I read.

*Quelle **veste** as-tu achetée?*
Which **jacket** did you buy?

*Combien de **glaces** a-t-elle prises?*
How many **ice-creams** did she have?

Point to watch

The past participle never agrees with an **indirect** object,

e.g. *Je **leur** ai envoyé une carte postale.*
I sent **them** a postcard. (**to them**)

*Il **nous** a montré la photo.*
He showed **us** the photo. (**to us**)

*Anne **lui** a acheté des bonbons.*
Anne bought **her** some sweets. (**for her**)

Q 33.3 Write in French.

a She lost it (a key). (*perdre, une clé*)

_____

_____

b We wrote them (postcards). (*écrire*: irregular past
participle!, *des cartes postales*)

_____

_____

c I bought it (the present). (*acheter, le cadeau*)

_____

_____

d They gave them (the flowers). (*donner, les fleurs*)

_____

_____

e How many exercises did you (sing., informal) do? (*faire*: irregular past participle!)

_____

_____

The perfect tense with *être*:

16 common verbs require *être* as the auxiliary verb. 12 of these can best be remembered as opposites:

		Perfect tense form
aller	to go	*je suis allé*
venir	to come	*je suis venu*
arriver	to arrive	*je suis arrivé*
partir	to leave	*je suis parti*
entrer	to go in	*je suis entré*
sortir	to leave, go out	*je suis sorti*
monter	to go up, to get on, into (transport)	*je suis monté*
descendre	to go down, to get off, out of (transport)	*je suis descendu*
naître	to be born	*je suis né*
mourir	to die	*je suis mort*
rester	to stay	*je suis resté*
retourner	to return	*je suis retourné*
tomber	to fall	*je suis tombé*

Three more are <u>compounds</u> of these verbs: *devenir* (to become); *revenir* (to come back); *rentrer* (to go back in, to go home). Any other compounds of these verbs would also require *être*, e.g. *repartir*; *ressortir*; *remonter*; *redescendre*; all meaning **to … again**.

Point to watch

Some of the past participles above are **irregular**.

The past participle of any verb formed with *être* must agree with its subject. The agreement is the same as adjectival agreement:

arriver

je suis arrivé(e) I have arrived, I arrived	*nous sommes arrivé(e)s*
tu es arrivé(e)	*vous êtes arrivé(e)(s)*
il est arrivé	*ils sont arrivés*
elle est arrivée	*elles sont arrivées*

The possible alternative agreements are quoted in brackets above,

e.g. *vous êtes arrivé* when referring to a man
vous êtes arrivée when referring to a woman
vous êtes arrivés when referring to more than one man or a mixed group
vous êtes arrivées when referring to more than one woman

Questions

Examples of question types **iii**, **iv** and **v** (see unit 28):

Est-ce que *Est-ce qu'il est parti?*
Intonation *Il est parti*   } Has he left?/Did he leave?
Inversion *Est-il parti? ***

*NB The auxiliary verb only is inverted.

The negative

Wrap **ne...pas** (etc) around the auxiliary verb,

e.g. *Je **ne** suis **pas** sorti(e).*
I have**n't** been out/did**n't** go out.

*Nous **ne** sommes **pas** resté(e)s avant.*
We have**n't** stayed/did**n't** stay before.

*Ils **ne** sont **pas** arrivés.*
They have**n't** arrived/did**n't** arrive.

Q 33.4 **Write in French.**

a I was born on .... (*naître*: irregular past participle!)

_____

_____

b He left at 3 p.m. (*partir*)

_____

_____

c   We (mixed group) arrived on Monday. (*arriver*)

_____

_____

d   The girls went out. (*sortir*)

_____

_____

e   Anne did not stay. (*rester*)

_____

_____

f   The footballer (male) fell. (*tomber*)

_____

_____

g   The men came to the office.
    (*venir*: irregular past participle!)

_____

_____

h   She has become a policewoman.
    (*devenir*: irregular past participle!)

_____

_____

i   You (sing.; informal; female) have never gone into the
    Louvre. (*entrer*)

_____

_____

j   Have you (sing.; formal; female) been back? (*retourner*)

_____

_____

Point to watch

Passer, when used to mean **to call round,** belongs to the group of verbs formed with **être,**

e.g. *Je suis passé(e) te voir hier.*
I called round/dropped by to see you yesterday.

but: *J'ai passé le livre à Michel.*
I passed the book to Michel.

Point to watch

The verbs **descendre, monter, rentrer** and **sortir** can be used with a direct object. In this case, they are formed using **avoir:**

e.g. *Il est descendu.*	He went/ has gone down(stairs).
but: *Il a descendu les ordures.*	He took the rubbish down.
Nous sommes montés.	We went up(stairs).
but: *Nous avons monté la valise.*	We took the case up.
Je suis rentré(e).	I went back in.
but: *J'ai rentré le linge.*	I brought the washing in.
Tu es sorti(e).	You went out, left.
but: *Tu as sorti les clefs.*	You took the keys out.

Q 33.5   Write in French.

a We (mixed group) went back in. (*rentrer*)

_____

_____

b She took the passport out. (*sortir*)

_____

_____

c The porter took the luggage downstairs. (*descendre*)

_____

_____

> **d** Christine and Florence got on the bus. (*monter*)
>
> _____
>
> _____

Reflexive verbs

You must use *être* for all reflexive verbs when forming the perfect tense. Therefore, the past participle will agree with its subject:

se laver

je me suis lavé(e) I washed myself	*nous nous sommes lavé(e)s*
tu t'es lavé(e)	*vous vous êtes lavé(e)(s)*
il s'est lavé	*ils se sont lavés*
elle s'est lavée	*elles se sont lavées*

Questions

Examples of question types **iii**, **iv** and **v** (see unit 28):

Est-ce que	*Est-ce qu'il s'est dépêché?*	
Intonation	*Il s'est dépêché?*	} Did he hurry?/Has he hurried?
Inversion	*S'est-il dépêché?*	

The negative

Wrap *ne...pas* (etc) around the auxiliary verb,

> e.g. *Je **ne** me suis **pas** endormi.*
> I have**n't** fallen asleep/did**n't** fall asleep.
>
> *Nous **ne** nous sommes **pas** levé(e)s.*
> We have**n't** got up/did**n't** get up.
>
> *Ils **ne** se sont **jamais** rappelés.*
> They have **never** remembered/did**n't** remember.

Point to watch

There are two cases when no agreement is made with the subject:

when there is a **direct object**:

> *Elle s'est lavé **les cheveux**.* → She washed **her hair**.
> (**Her hair** is the direct object.)

and when the reflexive pronoun becomes an **indirect object**:

> *Vous **vous** êtes parlé.* → You have spoken **to each other**.
> *Elles **se** sont téléphoné.* → They phoned **each other**.

Q 33.6 **Write in French.**

a The girls got up at 8.30. (*se lever*)

_____

_____

b We (mixed group) got some information at the Town
Hall. (*se renseigner*)

_____

_____

c I (male) went to bed late. (*se coucher*)

_____

_____

d Have you (sing.; informal; female) been bathing in the
sea? (*se baigner*)

_____

_____

e What happened? (*se passer*)

_____

_____

f Did you (pl.; mixed group) have a good time?
(*bien s'amuser*)

_____

_____

34 The imperfect tense

How to recognise the imperfect tense in English

The imperfect tense is used to express what **was** happen**ing** or **used to**
happen in the past, and for descriptions in the past. Some examples in
English:

> It **was raining**.
> We **were reading** a magazine.
> I **used to play** badminton.
> He **was wearing** a long coat.

Do not try to translate separately into French **was/were/used to** in the sentences above. The key ideas are **rain; read; play; wear.**

How to form the imperfect tense in French

Use the **present tense** *nous* form (minus *-ons*) as the stem.

Add the following endings to the stem:

(je)	*-ais*
(tu)	*-ais*
(il/elle/on)	*-ait*
(nous)	*-ions*
(vous)	*-iez*
(ils/elles)	*-aient*

e.g. **Nous form** → **stem** + **ending**

(il) *regardons* → *regard* **ait** → *Il regard***ait** *le château.*
(He **was looking** at the castle.)

(vous) finissons → *finiss* **iez** → *Vous finiss***iez** *l'exercice.*
(You **were finishing** the exercise.)

(elles) entendons → *entend* **aient** → *Elles entend***aient** *le chien.*
(They **used to hear** the dog.)

With the exception of the *nous* and *vous* forms, all the endings sound identical.

The importance of using the present tense *nous* form as your starting point shows up particularly with *-ir* verbs and irregulars:

Infinitive	Nous form	→	stem	Imperfect
choisir	*choisissons*	→	*choisiss*	→ *Je **choisissais** une magazine.* (I **was choosing** a magazine.)
lire	*lisons*	→	*lis*	→ *Nous **lisions** une annonce.* (We **were reading** an advert.)
faire	*faisons*	→	*fais*	→ *Tu **faisais** la vaisselle.* (You **were** washing up.)

être is the only irregular verb in the imperfect tense. Its stem is *ét-* but it takes <u>the same endings</u> as regular verbs:

j'étais	I was
tu étais	you (singular) were
il/elle/on était	he/she/it/one was
nous étions	we were
vous étiez	you (plural or polite singular form) were
ils/elles étaient	they were

Remember that some *-er* verbs undergo a spelling change in the present tense to maintain pronunciation (see page 60), e.g. *manger* and *commencer*:

Infinitive		*Nous* **form**		**imperfect stem**
manger	to eat	*mangeons*	→	*mange-*
nager	to swim	*nageons*	→	*nage-*
commencer	to start	*commençons*	→	*commenç-*

The *e* and the *ç* are also necessary in the imperfect tense:

> *Je mangeais une pomme.*
> *Tu mangeais une poire.*
> *Il mangeait une banane.*
> but: *Nous mangions des cerises.* (since *gi* gives a soft *g* sound)
> and: *Vous mangiez des raisins.*
> *Ils mangeaient un ananas.*

> *Je/Tu commençais à huit heures.*
> *Il commençait à huit heures et demie.*
> but: *Nous commencions à neuf heures.* (since *ci* is soft)
> and: *Vous commenciez à neuf heures dix.*
> *Ils commençaient plus tard.*

When to use the imperfect tense:

a In descriptions in the past:

Il faisait du soleil.	It **was** sunny.

L'homme portait un jean.
The man **was wearing** (or **wore**) jeans.

Elle avait les cheveux bruns.	She **had** brown hair.
C'était le deux mars.	It **was** the 2nd of March.

b To describe repeated or habitual actions in the past, where in English you might find **used to** or **would**:

Il venait le vendredi.	He **used to** come on Fridays.

Elle attendait au coin de la rue.
She **would** wait on the corner of the road.

Point to watch

The two examples above could also be expressed in English by using the simple past,

> e.g.   *Il ven**ait** le vendredi.*   He **came** on Fridays.
>
> *Elle attend**ait** au coin de la rue.*
> She **waited** on the corner of the road.

However, if you know that a repeated or habitual action is being described, you must use the imperfect tense in French.

Point to watch

If you can <u>not</u> replace **would** with **used to**, you need to use the conditional,

> e.g.   I **would** like an ice-cream, please.   = conditional
> He **would** believe the story now.   = conditional

Similarly, if you can <u>not</u> replace **could** with **was/were able to**, you need to use the conditional,

> e.g.   *Elle **pouvait** rendre visite quand elle voulait.*
> She **could** visit when she liked.   = imperfect tense
>
> but: He **could** do it tomorrow.   = conditional
> They **could** visit next year.   = conditional

c   To describe what **was happening**:

> *Il buv**ait** du vin.*   He **was drinking** wine.
> *Nous écriv**ions** des cartes postales.*   We **were writing** postcards.

Point to watch

The perfect and imperfect tenses contrast where the imperfect verb describes what **was happening** when the perfect verb **happened**. The imperfect verb is setting the scene when the action of the perfect verb cuts in,

> e.g.   *Il **buvait** du vin quand le téléphone **a sonné**.*
> He **was drinking** wine when the 'phone **rang**.
>
> *Nous **écrivions** des cartes postales quand la serveuse **est arrivé**.*
> We **were writing** postcards when the waitress **arrived**.

Reflexive verbs

With reflexive verbs, remember to include the correct reflexive pronoun (see unit 29),

> e.g. *Nous nous détend**ions** dans le jardin.*
> We **used to relax** in the garden./
> We **were relaxing** in the garden.
>
> *Je me demand**ais** si c'était vrai.*
> I **was wondering** if it were true./
> I **used to wonder** if it were true.

Questions

Examples of question types **iii**, **iv** and **v** (see unit 28):

> **Est-ce que**) *Est-ce qu'il jouait?*
> **Intonation** *Il jouait?*
> **Inversion** *Jouait-il?*
>
> Was he playing?/
> Did he used to play?

The negative

Wrap *ne...pas* (etc) around the verb,

> e.g. *Tu **ne** nageais **jamais**.* You **never** used to swim.
> *Elles **n'**écoutaient **pas**.* They weren**'t** listening.

Q 34 Write in French.

a You (pl.) were living in Lille at the time. (*habiter*)

_____

_____

b We used to know the Murier family. (*connaitre*: irregular in present tense!)

_____

_____

c The robber was tall... (*être*: irregular!)

_____

_____

d ... he was wearing a white jacket... (*porter*)

_____

_____

e ... he drove a Citroën.
(*conduire*: irregular in present tense!)

_____

_____

f Her name was Christine. (*s'appeler*)

_____

_____

g The girls never used to leave early. (*partir*: irregular in
present tense!)

_____

_____

h Were you (sing.; informal) waiting? (*attendre*)

_____

_____

i We were playing cards. (*jouer*)

_____

_____

j When I was young, I didn't often swim.
(*être*: irregular!; *nager*)

_____

_____

35 Two special constructions in the imperfect tense: *VENIR DE* and *DEPUIS*

French uses an imperfect tense verb in certain constructions where, in English, a pluperfect tense is used.

Venir (imperfect) *de* (+ infintive)   **Had just done** something

Compare the English and French in these phrases:

Imperfect tense verb in French	Pluperfect tense verb in English
*Je **venais** de recevoir ta lettre.*	I **had just** received your letter.
*Nous **venions** d'arriver.*	We **had just** arrived.

How to use **venir de**

Use the <u>imperfect tense</u> of **venir**.

The action verb (**what** has just been done) must be in the <u>infinitive</u> (this ends in either *-er*, *-re*, or *-ir*) e.g. *manger, perdre, choisir.*

Q 35.1 **Write in French.**

a He had just written to his friend. (*écrire*)

_____

_____

b The students (mixed group) had just finished the exam. (*finir*)

_____

_____

c The manager had just started the meeting. (*commencer*)

_____

_____

d We had just won the match. (*gagner*)

_____

_____

e The train had just left. (*sortir*

_____

_____

Point to watch

Using the imperfect tense of **venir de** + infinitive translates **had (just done)**. If you want to say **has** or **have (just done)** see unit 25, p. 60.

Depuis since/for (+ time phrase)

Compare the English and French in these phrases:

Imperfect tense verb in French	**Pluperfect tense verb in English**
J'habitais ici depuis un an.	I **had lived** here for a year.
*Il **apprenait** le français depuis 1997.*	He **had been learning** French since 1990.
*Nous **attendions** depuis vingt minutes.*	We'd **been waiting** for twenty minutes.

How to use *depuis*

Use the <u>imperfect tense</u> of the French verb where, in English, we use a pluperfect tense.

Q 35.2   Write in French.

a They had worked at the town hall for three years. (*travailler*)

_____

_____

b She had been studying chemistry for six months. (*étudier*)

_____

_____

c We had been swimming since 10.00. (*nager*)

_____

_____

d He had been an actor since the age of twelve. (*être*: irregular!)

_____

_____

e My brother had been playing basketball for half an hour. (*jouer*)

_____

_____

Point to watch

Using the imperfect tense with *depuis* translates **had (done/been doing)**. If you want to say **have** or **has (done/been doing)** see unit 25, p. 60.

36 The pluperfect tense

How to recognise the pluperfect tense in English

The pluperfect tense is used to express what **had** happen**ed** or **had been** happen**ing** in the past. Look out also for the contracted forms. Some examples in English:

I **had phoned** the hospital.	(contracted form: I'**d phoned** the hospital.)
He **had learned** French at school.	(contracted form: He'**d learned** French … .)
We **had been** listening.	(contracted form: We'**d been** listening.)

Point to watch

The pluperfect is used to position actions or events **further back in the past** than other actions or events in the past

> e.g. We **had booked** in January. (We went on holiday in July.)
> They **had promised** last week (to come to his party yesterday).

Point to watch

It is also used for reported speech in the past:

Direct speech	**Reported speech**
'Antoine visited the castle.'	He said that Antoine had visited the castle.

How to form the pluperfect tense in French

The pluperfect tense is made up of two parts:

the imperfect tense of the auxiliary verb + the past participle

> e.g. *Nous avions **reservé** en janvier.*
> We had booked in January.
>
> *Ils avaient **promis** la semaine dernière.*
> They had promised last week.
>
> *Il a dit qu'Antoine **avait visité** le château*
> He said that Antoine had visited the castle.

Points to watch

This tense is formed in the same way as the perfect tense, except that the auxiliary verb is used in the imperfect tense. All the rules regarding whether to use *avoir* or *être* as the auxiliary; preceding direct object agreement; agreement of the past participle with the subject and how to form questions and negatives apply in exactly the same way (see unit 33).

The pluperfect tense with avoir:

j'avais visité I **had** visited
tu avais visité
il/elle/on avait visité
nous avions visité
vous aviez visité
ils/elles avaient visité

The pluperfect tense with être:

j'étais arrivé(e) I **had** arrived
tu étais arrivé(e)
il/elle/on était arrivé(e)
nous étions arrivé(e)s
vous étiez arrivé(e)(s)
ils/elles étaient arrivé(e)s

The pluperfect tense with reflexive verbs:

je m'étais couché(e) I **had** gone to bed
tu t'étais couché(e)
il/elle/on s'était couché(e)
nous nous étions couché(e)s
vous vous étiez couché(e)(s)
ils/elles s'étaient couché(e)s

Point to watch

If the action is incomplete at this point in the past (e.g. he had lived there for five years – **and was still living there**), then you need to use a different construction in French, using *depuis* (see unit 35, p. 108).

Point to watch

If you want to say that an action had **just** occurred, you need to use a different construction in French using *venir de* (see unit 35, p. 107).

Q 36 **Write in French.**

1. He had forgotten the address. (*oublier*)

_____

_____

b Isabelle had finished the exercise. (*finir*)

_____

_____

c I had been playing tennis. (*jouer*)

_____

_____

d They (mixed group) had arrived early. (*arriver*)

_____

_____

e It had been raining. (*pleuvoir*: irregular past participle!)

_____

_____

f My parents had sold the car. (*vendre*)

_____

_____

g The waitresses had left. (*partir*)

_____

_____

h The tourists had got up at 5 a.m. (*se lever*)

_____

_____

i Had you (sing. formal, female) seen the accident?
(*voir*: irregular past participle!)

_____

_____

j We had bought nothing. (*acheter*)

_____

_____

37 Common irregular verbs

Here is a list of some common irregular French verbs. There are others, which can be found in a good dictionary, but these are the main ones you will need to take you to G.C.S.E. level.

Remember that compounds of these verbs will have similar forms,

e.g. ***venir*** and its compounds *de**venir*** and *re**venir***

prendre and its compounds *com**prendre*** and *sur**prendre***

Infinitive	Command	Present	Future	Perfect	Imperfect
aller (to go)	va allez allons	je vais; tu vas il/elle/on va nous allons vous allez ils/elles vont	j'irai	je suis allé(e)	j'allais
appeler (to call)	appelle appelez appelons	j'appelle tu appelles il/elle/on appelle nous appelons vous appelez ils/elles appellent	j'appelerai	j'ai appelé	j'appelais
s'asseoir (to sit down)	assieds-toi asseyez-vous asseyons-nous	je m'assieds tu t'assieds il/elle/on s'assied nous nous asseyons vous vous asseyez ils/elles s'asseyent	je m'assiérai	je me suis assis(e)	je m'asseyais
avoir (to have)	aie ayez ayons	j'ai; tu as il/elle/on a nous avons vous avez ils/elles ont	j'aurai	j'ai eu	j'avais
boire (to drink)	bois buvez buvons	je bois; tu bois il/elle/on boit nous buvons vous buvez ils/elles boivent	je boirai	j'ai bu	je buvais
conduire (to lead)	conduis conduisez conduisons	je conduis tu conduis il/elle/on conduit nous conduisons vous conduisez ils conduisent elles conduisent	je conduirai	j'ai conduit	je conduisais

Infinitive	Command	Present	Future	Perfect	Imperfect
connaître (to know)	connais connaissez connaissons	je connais tu connais il/elle/on connaît nous connaissons vous connaissez ils connaissent elles connaissent	je connaîtrai	j'ai connu	je connaissais
courir (to run)	cours courez courons	je cours; tu cours il/elle/on court nous courons vous courez ils/elles courent	je courrai	j'ai couru	je courais
croire (to believe)	crois croyez croyons	je crois; tu crois il/elle/on croit nous croyons vous croyez ils/elles croient	je croirai	j'ai cru	je croyais
devoir (to owe) (to have to) (must)	dois devez devons	je dois; tu dois il/elle/on doit nous devons vous devez ils/elles doivent	je devrai	j'ai dû	je devais
dire (to say) (to tell)	dis dites disons	je dis; tu dis il/elle/on dit nous disons vous dites ils/elles disent	je dirai	j'ai dit	je disais
dormir (to sleep)	dors dormez dormons	je dors; tu dors il/elle/on dort nous dormons vous dormez ils/elles dorment	je dormirai	j'ai dormi	je dormais
écrire (to write)	écris écrivez écrivons	j'écris; to écris il/elle/on écrit nous écrivons vous écrivez ils/elles écrivent	j'écrirai	j'ai écrit	j'écrivais
envoyer (to send)	envoie envoyez envoyons	j'envoie tu envoies il/elle/on envoie nous envoyons vous envoyez ils/elles envoient	j'enverrai	j'ai envoyé	j'envoyais

Infinitive	Command	Present	Future	Perfect	Imperfect
être (to be)	sois soyez soyons	je suis, tu es il/elle/on est nous sommes vous êtes ils/elles sont	je serai	j'ai été	j'étais
faire (to do) (to make)	fais faites faisons	je fais, tu fais il/elle/on fait nous faisons vous faites ils/elles font	je ferai	j'ai fait	je faisais
falloir (to be necessary)		il faut	il faudra	il a fallu	il fallait
lire (to read)	lis lisez lisons	je lis, tu lis il/elle/on lit nous lisons vous lisez ils/elles lisent	je lirai	j'ai lu	je lisais
mettre (to put)	mets mettez mettons	je mets, tu mets il/elle/on met nous mettons vous mettez ils/elles mettent	je mettrai	j'ai mis	je mettais
mourir (to die)	meurs mourez mourons	je meurs, tu meurs il/elle/on meurt nous mourons vous mourez ils/elles meurent	je mourrai	je suis mort(e)	je mourais
naître (to be born)		il/elle/on naît ils/elles naissent	il/elle naîtra ils/elles naîtront	je suis né(e)	je naissais
offrir (to offer)	offree offrez offrons	j'offre; tu offres il/elle/on offre nous offrons vous offrez ils/elles offrent	j'offrirai	j'ai offert	j'offrais
ouvrir (to open)	ouvre ouvrez ouvrons	j'ouvre; tu ouvres il/elle/on ouvre nous ouvrons vous ouvrez ils/elles ouvrent	j'ouvrirai	j'ai ouvert	j'ouvrais
partir (to leave)	pars partez partons	je pars; tu pars il/elle/on part nous partons vous partez ils/elles partent	je partirai	je suis parti(e)	je partais

Infinitive	Command	Present	Future	Perfect	Imperfect
pleuvoir (to rain)		il pleut	il pleuvra	il a plu	il pleuvait
pouvoir (to be able) (can)		je peux (je puis) tu peux il/elle/on peut nous pouvons vous pouvez ils/elles peuvent	je pourrai	j'ai pu	je pouvais
prendre (to take)	prends prenez prenons	je prends tu prends il/elle/on prend nous prenons vous prenez ils/elles prennent	je prendrai	j'ai pris	je prenais
recevoir (to receive)	reçois recevez recevons	je reçois tu reçois il/elle/on reçoit nous recevons vous recevez ils reçoivent elles reçoivent	je recevrai	j'ai reçu	je recevais
rire (to laugh)	ris riez rions	je ris, tu ris il/elle/on rit nous rions vous riez ils/elles rient	je rirai	j'ai ri	je riais
savoir (to know)	sache sachez sachons	je sais, tu sais il/elle/on sait nous savons vous savez ils/elles savent	je saurai	j'ai su	je savais
(se) sentir (to feel)	sens sentez sentons	je (me) sens; tu (te) sens il/elle/on (se) sent nous (nous) sentons vous (vous) sentez ils/elles (se) sentent	je (me) sentirai	j'ai senti je me suis senti(e)	je (me) sentais
servir (to serve)	sers servez servons	je sers; tu sers il/elle/on sert nous servons vous servez ils/elles servent	je servirai	j'ai servi	je servais
sortir (to go out) (to come out) (to leave)	sors sortez sortons	je sors; tu sors il/elle/on sort nous sortons vous sortez ils/elles sortent	je sortirai	je suis sorti(e)	je sortais

Infinitive	Command	Present	Future	Perfect	Imperfect
suivre to follow	suis suivez suivons	je suis; tu suis il/elle/on suit nous suivons vous suivez ils/elles suivent	je suivrai	j'ai suivi	je suivais
venir (to come)	viens venez venons	je viens; tu viens il/elle/on vient nous venons vous venez ils/elles viennent	je viendrai	je suis venu(e)	je venais
vivre (to live)	vis vivez vivons	je vis; tu vis il/elle/on vit nous vivons vous vivez ils/elles vivent	je vivrai	j'ai vécu	je vivais
voir (to see)	vois voyez voyons	je vois; tu vois il/elle/on voit nous voyons vous voyez ils/elles voient	je verrai	j'ai vu	je voyais
vouloir (to want)	veuille veuillez veuillons	je veux; tu veux il/elle/on veut nous voulons vous voulez ils/elles veulent	je voudrai	j'ai voulu	je voulais

Answers

Q 1

a Minister
b came
c French
d unexpectedly
e him
f in
g flight Minister London
h and

Q 2

a un chat, une maison, un champ, un garçon, une fille, une pomme, un œuf
b Il vend à un supermarché et à une boulangerie.
c le jardin d'une maison
le jardin d'un château.
d Je suis professeur.
e cent stylos et mille crayons

Q 3

a
le stylo	le crayon	la sœur
la fille	le fils	la fenêtre
l'ami(e)	l'enfant	l'hôtel
les stylos	les sœurs	les ami(e)s
les hôtels		

b Les chats sont intéressants mais les chiens sont plus intéressants.
c Le français est la langue de la Belgique.
d Elle a les cheveux longs.
e La Reine Elisabeth.
f Je vais au cinéma. Je vais à l'hôtel. Je vais aux magasins. Je vais à la boucherie.
g le stylo de l'homme
le stylo de la femme
le stylo du garçon
les stylos des garçons

Q 4

a J'achète du pain, du vin, de la viande, de la confiture, de l'eau et des pommes.
b Je mange un peu de viande et beaucoup de fruit.
c Je voudrais un litre d'huile et 500 grammes de fromage.
d Je veux du café mais je ne veux pas de lait.

e J' ai de l'argent mais je n'ai pas de voiture.
f Je vois des touristes mais je ne vois pas d'étudiants.

Q 5

a le cousin – cousin
b la cousine – cousin
c le propiétaire (man) – owner
d la propiétaire (woman) – owner
e le chef – boss
f le lundi – Monday
g l'été (masc.) – summer
h l'espagnol (masc.) – Spanish
i le sud – South
j le canotage – canoeing
k le bain – bath
l le rideau – curtain
m le conducteur – driver
n le mécanicien – mechanic
o le sanglier – boar
p le changement – change
q le pouvoir – power
r la distance – distance
s la journée – day
t la négligence – negligence
u la chaussette – sock
v la maladie – illness
w la distraction – distraction
x un livre et une livre
y un poste à la poste
z un tour de la tour

Q 6

1 le temps, les temps
2 la voix, les voix
3 le nez, les nez
4 le trou, les trous
5 le pneu, les pneus
6 l'animal, les animaux
7 le bijou, les bijoux
8 le bois, les bois
9 le caillou, les cailloux
10 le chapeau, les chapeaux
11 le château, les châteaux
12 le cheval, les chevaux
13 le chou, les choux
14 le ciel, les cieux
15 l'eau, les eaux
16 le feu, les feux
17 le gâteau, les gâteaux
18 le genou, les genoux
19 le hibou, les hiboux
20 le jeu, les jeux

21 le journal, les journaux
22 le mal, les maux
23 l'œil, les yeux
24 l'oiseau, les oiseaux
25 l'os, les os
26 le prix, les prix
27 le tableau, les tableaux
28 le timbre-poste, les timbres-poste
29 le travail, les travaux
30 Mesdemoiselles! Mesdames! Messieurs!
31 Nous allons dîner chez les Smith.

Q 7

a   un livre brun
b   une chaise brune
c   deux livres bruns
d   deux chaises brunes
e   deux chaises énormes
f   deux garçons anglais
g   une fille paresseuse
h   deux garçons paresseux
i   un garçon actif
j   une fille active
k   une maison ancienne
l   une chemise chère
m   une situation pareille

Q 8

a   un plafond bas
b   une belle femme
c   deux maisons blanches
d   une tranche épaisse
e   la famille entière
f   une matière favorite
g   deux fraises fraîches
h   une grosse chatte
i   deux grasses boîtes
j   une longue promenade
k   une voiture neuve
l   une serviette sèche
m   une vieille histoire
n   une fille vive
o   un nouvel ami

Q 9

a   un excellent match
b   un jeune homme
c   un mauvais garçon
d   la même chose
e   son meilleur ami
f   un petit verre
g   le vieux pont
h   mon cher neveu
i   ma voiture chère

j   ma propre maison
k   ma maison propre

Q 10

a   un autre ami
b   Chaque enfant a le même livre.
c   plusieurs fois
d   quelques livres
e   De tels enfants sont rares.
f   toutes les nièces et tous les neveux

Q 11

a   La voiture verte est plus grande que la voiture bleue.
b   La voiture bleue est moins chère.
c   La voiture rouge est la plus grande.
d   La voiture blanche est aussi chère que la voiture verte.
e   La voiture grise est la moins chère.
f   La voiture rouge est la plus chère.
g   La meilleur voiture est une voiture française.
h   Les voitures françaises sont meilleurs que les voitures anglaises.
i   La chose la plus importante est le prix.
j   Les voitures françaises sont les meilleures du monde.

Q 12

a   cette chaise
b   ce chien
c   cet ami
d   cette amie
e   ces chaises
f   cette chaise-ci
g   cette chaise-là
h   ces chaises-ci
i   ces chaises-là

Q 13

a   mon chien
b   mes chiens
c   ma chaise
d   mon idée
e   ton chien
f   tes chiens
g   ta chaise
h   ton intention
i   son chien
j   son chien
k   ses chiens
l   ses chiens
m   notre voiture
n   nos voitures

o   votre voiture
p   vos voitures
q   leur maison
r   leurs maisons

Q 14

a   Quel chien?
b   Quels chiens?
c   Quelle page?
d   Quelles pages?
e   Quel est ton nom?
f   Quel est ton número de téléphone?
g   Quel dommage!

Q 15

a   Il marche lentement.
b   Il marche silencieusement.
c   Heureusement il était là.
d   C'était entièrement de sa faute.
e   Il parle poliment.
f   Il parle vite.
g   Il a trop bu.
h   Il a souvent parlé de son enfance.

Q 16

a   Il s'est couché car il était fatigué.
b   Il joue comme son frère.
c   Il était fatigué donc il s'est couché.
d   Quand il arrivera je le lui dirai.
e   Il est triste parce qu'il a perdu son argent.
f   Pendant que je regardais la télé, les cambrioleurs sont entrés.
g   J'ai joué au tennis tandis que Paul est resté au lit.

Q 17

a   A peu près vingt voitures.
b   Il a téléphoné au sujet de (à propos de) vos vacances.
c   Il commencera à trois heures environ.
d   Il s'est promené le long de la plage.
e   Il a distribué l'argent parmi ses amis.
f   Il est parti avant la fin du repas.
g   Je l'ai déjà fait.
h   Je serai devant le cinéma.
i   Il a voyagé à vélo et en voiture.
j   La boulangerie est près de la gare.
k   J'habite ici depuis cinq ans.
l   J'étudiais le français depuis dix ans.
m   J'y suis resté pendant une heure.
n   Je serai en Espagne pour une semaine.
o   A Paris les jupes courtes sont à la mode.
p   Quand vous arriverez en France vous serez au centre-ville en une heure.

q   A son retour en France il a roulé à gauche.
r   Il a pris sa cravate dans une armoire.
s   Il était maintenant hors de danger.
t   Par la fenêtre j'ai vu le voleur.
u   L'horloge est par-dessus de la porte.
v   plus de dix
w   Il a dormi depuis dix heures.
x   Il a dormi jusqu'à dix heures.
y   Il est entré en courant.
z   Il est sorti en courant.

Q 18

a   Il m'aide.
b   Il t'aide.
c   Il l'aide.
d   Il l'aide.
e   Il nous aide.
f   Il vous aide.
g   Il les aide.
h   Il m'écrit.
i   Il t'écrit.
j   Il lui écrit.
k   Il lui écrit.
l   Il nous écrit.
m   Il vous écrit.
n   Il leur écrit.
o   Il le lui donne.
p   Donnez-le-lui.
q   Ils ne les leur donne pas.
r   Ne les leur donnez pas.
s   Je l'y ai vu.
t   J'en ai deux.

Q 19

a   Ces livres sont les miens and ces crayons sont les tiens.
b   Ce livre est le mien et cette chaise est la tienne.
c   Le livre est le sien et la voiture est la sienne.
d   Le livre est le sien et la voiture est la sienne.
e   L'argent est le nôtre et les livres sont les nôtres.
f   La chaise est la vôtre et les livres sont les vôtres.
g   La maison est la leur et les stylos sont les leurs.

Q 20

a   Voici des sacs. Celui qui est à gauche est bleu. Ceux qui sont sur la table sont verts.

b   Voici des chemises. Celle qui est à gauche est bleue. Celles qui sont sur la table sont vertes.

c   Voici des maillots de bain. Celui-ci est bleu et celui-là est rouge.

d   Voici deux vestes. Celle-ci est bleue et celle-là est rouge.

e   Voici des gants. Ceux-ci sont rouges et ceux-là sont bleus.

f   Voici des lunettes de soleil. Celles-ci sont rouges et celles-là sont bleues.

g   Ceci est bon et cela est mauvais.

Q 21

a   Le cadeau est pour moi.
b   Le cadeau est pour toi.
c   Le cadeau est pour lui.
d   Le cadeau est pour elle.
e   Le cadeau est pour nous.
f   Le cadeau est pour vous.
g   Le cadeau est pour eux.
h   Le cadeau est pour elles.
i   Je l'ai fait moi-même.
j   Elle l'a fait elle-même.
k   Lui, il l'a fait, pas moi.
l   Qui est le coupable? Toi!
m   Qui est le coupable? C'est moi.

Q 22

a   Le livre que j'ai lu est sur la table.
b   L'homme qui a écrit le livre est à la table.
c   Le livre dont il parle est sur la table.
d   Je ne me rappelle pas ce que j'ai vu.
e   Je ne sais pas ce qui est arrivé.
f   Voici des gâteaux.
Lequel voulez-vous?
Lesquels voulez-vous?
g   Voici des pommes.
Laquelle voulez-vous?
Lesquelles voulez-vous?

Q 23

a   Où sont les autres?
b   Chacun est très cher.
c   Elle sort avec n'importe qui.
d   Tu peux prendre n'importe quoi.
e   Tu peux y aller n'importe quel jour.
f   J'y ai été plusieurs fois.
g   Il y a quelqu'un en bas.
h   Quelques-unes des assiettes étaient sales.
i   Tout est normal.
j   Tout le monde est allé à la boum.

Q 24.1

a   Elle prépare le déjeuner.
b   Il cherche la maison.
c   Je mange le fromage.
d   Nous habitons (à) Newcastle.
e   Ils marchent vite.
f   Vous trouvez l'anglais facile.
g   J'habite au bord de la mer.
h   Vous chantez bien.
i   Nous regardons la télévision.
j   Il commence à 20 heures.

Q 24.2

a   Je choisis la voiture bleue.
b   Les enfants finissent leurs devoirs.
c   Tu remplis le réservoir.
d   Nous choisissons la carte.
e   Ils bâtissent un garage.

Q 24.3

a   J'attends le bus.
b   Frédérique entend le chien.
c   Nous rendons les livres.
d   Ils perdent le match.
e   Vous vendez les glaces.
f   Elle répond immédiatement.
g   Tu descends l'escalier.
h   Je pends le linge.
i   Elle vend la maison.
j   Ils rendent l'argent.

Q 24.4

a   Il va à Paris.
b   Anne a un chat.
c   Pierre est belge.
d   Nous sommes en Suisse.
e   Ils ont trois enfants.
f   Je vais en ville.
g   Vous allez en vacances.
h   Tu as le temps.
i   J'ai un rhume.
j   Paul et Jeanne sont dans le jardin.

Q 25.1

a   Il vient d'écrire à son ami(e).
b   Les étudiants viennent de finir l'examen.
c   Le directeur vient de commencer la réunion.
d   Mon équipe vient de gagner.
e   Vous venez de manquer l'avion.

Q 25.2

a   Ils travaillent à la Mairie/à l'Hôtel de Ville depuis trois ans.
b   Elle étudie la chimie depuis six mois.

c Nous nageons depuis dix heures.
d Il est acteur depuis l'âge de douze ans.
e Mon frère cherche le livre depuis une demi-heure.

Q 26.1
a Nous n'écoutons pas la radio.
b Ils ne jouent jamais au football.
c Elle n'achète rien.
d Je ne lave jamais la voiture.
e Marc ne mange guère.
f Ils ne mangent que des plats végétariens.
g Tu n'attends personne.
h Nous n'allons nulle part.
i Ils ne vendent plus le pain.
j Vous n'entendez aucun bruit.

Q 26.2
a Ils ne se couchent pas à vingt-deux heures.
b Elle ne se brosse jamais les dents.
c Ils ne s'appelent pas Jameau.
d Qui sait? Personne.
e Nous ne prêtons jamais rien.
f Qu'est-ce qu'il y a à la télévision? Rien.
g (Est-ce que) Tu ne joues pas de la guitarre? Si!
h Je n'ai pas de temps libre.
i C'est mardi, n'est-ce pas?
j Mes parents ne s'inquiètent jamais.

Q 27
a Ecoute!/Ecoutez!/Ecoutons!
b Dors!/Dormez!/Dormons!
c Arrête!/Arrêtez!/Arrêtons!
d Lance le ballon!/Lancez le ballon!/Lançons le ballon!
e Viens!/Venez!/Venons!
f Couche-toi!/Couchez-vous!/Couchons-nous!
g Ne te fâche pas!/Ne vous fâchez pas!/Ne nous fâchons pas!
h Va!/Allez!/Allons!
i Ne pars pas!/Ne partez pas!/Ne partons pas!
j Assieds-toi!/Asseyez-vous!/Asseyons-nous!

Q 28
a Qui habite ici?/Qui est-ce qui habite ici?
b Où travailles-tu?/Où est-ce que tu travailles?
c Quand allez-vous en vacances?/Quand est-ce que vous allez en vacances?

d Pourquoi sont-ils à Paris?/Pourquoi est-ce qu'ils sont à Paris?
e D'où vient le train?
f Tu étudies l'espagnol?/Est-ce que tu étudies l'espagnol?/(Etudies-tu l'espagnol? is possible, but unlikely.)
g Vous devez partir maintenant?/Est-ce que vous devez partir maintenant?/Devez-vous partir maintenant?
h Ils ont un ordinateur?/Est-ce qu'ils ont un ordinateur?/Ont-ils un ordinateur?
i Elle reste à l'hôtel/Est-ce qu'elle reste à l'hôtel?/Reste-t-elle à l'hôtel?
j Nous voulons participer?/Est-ce que nous voulons participer?/Voulons-nous participer?

Q 29
a Je m'appelle Giraud.
b Nous nous reposons.
c Virginie ne se détend jamais.
d Tu te coiffes.
e Vous vous promenez au bord de la mer?/Est-ce que vous vous promenez au bord de la mer?/Vous promenez-vous au bord de la mer?
f Je me demande.
g Ils vont se baigner dans la mer.
h Nous devons nous lever.
i Tu dois te réveiller à sept heures.
j Vous vous rasez vite.

Q 30.1
a Je regarderai la télé.
b Il ne jouera pas.
c Nous porterons le sac.
d Ils essayeront.
e Je sortirai ce soir.
f Le train partira à dix heures cinq.
g Elle restera à la maison.
h Ils n'attendront pas le bus.
i Tu perdras ton argent.
j Je ne me rappelerai pas.

Q 30.2
a Je serai à Paris la semaine prochaine.
b Tu ne verras pas le film.
c Ils voudront les billets?/Est-ce qu'ils voudront les billets?/Voudront-ils les billets?
d Nous irons vendredi.
e Papa fera la vaisselle.
f Elle saura demain.
g Ils enverront le fax.

h   Nous recevrons le fax cet après-midi.

i   Pierre n'aura pas assez de temps.

j   Vous pourrez aider?

k   Il pleuvra ce weekend.

l   Il faudra réserver une table?/Est-ce qu'il faudra réserver une table?/Faudra-t-il réserver une table? (or: Nous devrons réserver une table? etc.)

Q 30.3

a   Quand je téléphonerai, je laisserai un message.

b   Nous enverrons une carte postale quand nous serons en France.

c   Dès qu'ils auront les détails, ils réserveront.

d   Elle commencera à travailler aussitôt qu'elle recevra le contrat.

Q 31

a   Nous allons demander.

b   Ils vont participer.

c   Tu ne vas pas visiter la cathédrale.

d   Ils ne vont pas finir leurs devoirs aujourd'hui.

e   Elle va envoyer un fax.

f   Il va parler avec M. Lombard?/Est-ce qu'il va parler avec M. Lombard?/Va-t-il parler avec M. Lombard?

g   Nous allons chercher la clé?/Est-ce que nous allons chercher la clé?/Allons-nous chercher la clé?

h   Je vais travailler dans une banque.

i   Elle va se reposer.

j   Nous allons nous laver.

Q 32.1

a   Je travaillerais beaucoup.

b   Nous nagerions l'après-midi.

c   Helen jouerais au tennis.

d   Jean et Claudie rendraient visite à leurs parents.

e   Vous trouveriez facilement le village.

f   Il donnerait le cadeau à Michel.

g   Ils se souviendraient.

h   Je n'apprendrais pas beaucoup.

Q 32.2

a   Ils viendront.

b   Il devrait comprendre notre problème.

c   Nous irions directement à la côte.

d   Béatrice saurait la réponse.

e   Je voudrais voyager.

f   Tu pourrais essayer le pantalon.

g   La société enverrait les détails.

h   Vous auriez du temps libre.

i   Ma tante et mon oncle ne seraient pas là.

j   Elle le ferait.

Q 33.1

a   Elle a dépensé cent livres.

b   Vous avez travaillé dur.

c   Ils ont choisi le cadeau.

d   Ils ont rempli la valise?/Est-ce qu'ils ont rempli la valise?/Ont-ils rempli la valise?

e   Il a perdu son passeport.

f   J'ai répondu à la question.

g   Nous n'avons rien entendu.

h   Tu as dégusté les escargots?/Est-ce que tu as dégusté les escargots?/As-tu dégusté les escargots?

i   J'ai attendu l'autobus une demi-heure.

j   Nous n'avons pas passé longtemps sur la plage.

Q 33.2

a   M. Maillac a lu le journal.

b   Les enfants ont fait la vaisselle.

c   Nous n'avons pas reçu la lettre.

d   Vous avez pris un café?/Est-ce que vous avez pris un café?/Avez-vous pris un café?

e   Mon papa a conduit à la côte.

f   Nous avons bu du champagne au mariage.

g   Elle n'a pas eu la grippe.

h   J'ai été chez le médecin.

i   Tu as vu le film?/Est-ce que tu as vu le film?/As-tu vu le film?

j   J'ai mis le couvert.

Q 33.3

a   Elle l'a perdue.

b   Nous les avons écrites.

c   Je l'ai acheté. (no agreement)

d   Ils les ont données.

e   Combien d'exercices as-tu faits?

Q 33.4

a   Je suis né(e) le … .

b   Il est parti à 15 heures.

c   Nous sommes arrivés lundi.

d   Les filles sont sorties.

e   Anne n'est pas restée.

f   Le footballeur est tombé.

g   Les hommes sont venus au bureau.

h   Elle est devenue femme-agent.

i   Tu n'es jamais entrée dans le Louvre.

j   Vous êtes retournée au Louvre?/Est-ce
    que vous êtes retournée/Êtes-vous
    retournée

Q 33.5

a   Nous sommes rentrés.
b   Elle a sorti le passeport.
c   Le porteur a descendu les bagages.
d   Christine et Florence sont montées dans
    l'autobus.

Q 33.6

a   Les filles se sont levées à huit heures et
    demie.
b   Nous nous sommes renseignés à la
    Mairie./à l'Hôtel de Ville.
c   Je me suis couché tard.
d   Tu t'es baignée dans la mer?/Est-ce que
    tu t'es baignée dans la mer?/T'es-tu
    baignée dans la mer?
e   Qu'est-ce qui s'est passé?
f   Vous êtes-vous bien amusés?/Est-ce que
    vous vous êtes bien amusés?/Vous vous
    êtes bien amusés?

Q 34

a   Vous habitiez (à) Lille à l'époque.
b   Nous connaissions la famille Murier.
c   Le voleur était grand …
d   … il portait une veste blanche …
e   … il conduisait une Citroën.
f   Elle s'appelait Christine.
g   Les filles ne partaient jamais tôt.
h   Tu attendais?/Est-ce que tu attendais?/
    Attendais-tu?
i   Nous jouions aux cartes.
j   Quand j'étais jeune, je ne nageais pas
    souvent.

Q 35.1

a   Il venait décrire à son ami(e).
b   Les étudiants venaient de finir l'examen.
c   Le directeur venait de commencer
    la réunion.
d   Nous venions de gagner le match.
e   Le train venait de sortir.

Q 35.2

a   Ils travaillaient à la Mairie/à l'Hôtel
    de Ville depuis trois ans.
b   Elle étudiait la chimie depuis six mois.
c   Nous nagions depuis dix heures.
d   Il était acteur depuis l'âge de douze ans.
e   Mon frère jouait au basket depuis une
    demi-heure.

Q 36

a   Il avait oublié l'adresse.
b   Isabelle avait fini l'exercice.
c   J'avais joué au tennis.
d   Ils étaient arrivés tôt.
e   Il avait plu.
f   Mes parents avaient vendu la voiture.
g   Les serveuses étaient parties.
h   Les touristes s'étaient levés à 5 heures.
i   Vous aviez vu l'accident?/Est-ce que vous
    aviez vu? /Aviez-vous vu?
j   Nous n'avions rien acheté.